THE BEDFORD SERIES IN HISTORY AND CULTURE

Muckraking

Three Landmark Articles

The World Turned Upside Down: Indian Voices from Early America
Edited with an introduction by Colin G. Calloway, *University of Wyoming*

The Autobiography of Benjamin Franklin
Edited with an introduction by Louis P. Masur, *City University of New York*

Benjamin and William Franklin: Father and Son, Patriot and Loyalist
Sheila L. Skemp, *University of Mississippi*

Narrative of the Life of Frederick Douglass, An American Slave, Written by Himself
Edited with an introduction by David W. Blight, *Amherst College*

Muckraking: Three Landmark Articles
Edited with an introduction by Ellen F. Fitzpatrick, *Harvard University*

Plunkitt of Tammany Hall by William L. Riordon
Edited with an introduction by Terrence J. McDonald, *University of Michigan*

American Cold War Strategy: Interpreting NSC 68
Edited with an introduction by Ernest R. May, *Harvard University*

The Age of McCarthyism: A Brief History with Documents
Ellen Schrecker, *Yeshiva University*

Postwar Immigrant America: A Social History
Reed Ueda, *Tufts University*

THE BEDFORD SERIES IN HISTORY AND CULTURE

Muckraking

Three Landmark Articles

Edited with an introduction by

Ellen F. Fitzpatrick

Harvard University

BEDFORD BOOKS *of* ST. MARTIN'S PRESS

Boston · New York

For Bedford Books

Publisher: Charles H. Christensen
Associate Publisher/General Manager: Joan E. Feinberg
History Editor: Niels Aaboe
Developmental Editor: Louise D. Townsend
Managing Editor: Elizabeth M. Schaaf
Production Editor: Ann Sweeney
Copyeditor: Barbara G. Flanagan
Text Design: Claire Seng-Niemoeller
Cover Design: Richard Emery Design
Cover Art (left to right): Lincoln Steffens, Ida G. Tarbell, and Ray Stannard Baker. Ray Stannard Baker and Ida Tarbell courtesy of The Bettmann Archive, New York. Lincoln Steffens courtesy of Brown Brothers, Sterling, PA.

Library of Congress Catalog Card Number: 92-75888
Manufactured in the United States of America.

8   7   6   5   4

f   e   d   c   b   a

For information, write: St. Martin's Press, Inc., 175 Fifth Avenue, New York, NY 10010
Editorial Offices: Bedford Books *of* St. Martin's Press, 29 Winchester Street, Boston, MA 02116

ISBN: 0-312-08944-9 (paperback)
ISBN: 0-312-10280-1 (hardcover)

Acknowledgments

   Illustrations from the three *McClure's* articles are reprinted courtesy of the Trustees of the Boston Public Library.

Foreword

The Bedford Series in History and Culture is designed so that readers can study the past as historians do.

The historian's first task is finding the evidence. Documents, letters, memoirs, interviews, pictures, movies, novels, or poems can provide facts and clues. Then the historian questions and compares the sources. There is more to do than in a courtroom, for hearsay evidence is welcome, and the historian is usually looking for answers beyond act and motive. Different views of an event may be as important as a single verdict. How a story is told may yield as much information as what it says.

Along the way the historian seeks help from other historians and perhaps from specialists in other disciplines. Finally, it is time to write, to decide on an interpretation and how to arrange the evidence for readers.

Each book in this series contains an important historical document or group of documents, each document a witness from the past and open to interpretation in different ways. The documents are combined with some element of historical narrative—an introduction or a biographical essay, for example— that provides students with an analysis of the primary source material and important background information about the world in which it was produced.

Each book in the series focuses on a specific topic within a specific historical period. Each provides a basis for lively thought and discussion about several aspects of the topic and the historian's role. Each is short enough (and inexpensive enough) to be a reasonable one-week assignment in a college course. Whether as classroom or personal reading, each book in the series provides firsthand experience of the challenge—and fun—of discovering, recreating, and interpreting the past.

Natalie Zemon Davis
Ernest R. May

Preface

Ray Stannard Baker, Lincoln Steffens, and Ida Tarbell were three of the great American journalists of the twentieth century. Together with other passionately involved and deeply influential Progressive-era investigative reporters, they used their gifts as writers to illuminate the realities of the new American industrial society. Writing in early-twentieth-century mass-circulation magazines, these "muckrakers" managed simultaneously to enthrall, enrage, and, some would argue, empower their readers. They earned for their efforts both widespread acclaim and harsh criticism. Most important, they found an enduring place in history.

Muckraking was a pejorative term first hurled at the reporters' efforts by an exasperated President Theodore Roosevelt and then etched in stone by generations of historians who studied, puzzled over, and even marveled at the reporters' work without ever casting aside Roosevelt's epithet. Who were the muckrakers? What constituted muckraking? Why was investigative journalism so much a part of the intellectual, social, political, and cultural scene of the early twentieth century? What impact did muckraking have on Progressive politics and history? This book invites readers to explore these questions by reprinting three famous muckraking essays that appeared together in the January 1903 issue of *McClure's Magazine*. The introductory and concluding essays suggest ways of understanding muckraking.

Ray Stannard Baker's controversial piece on the anthracite coal strike, "The Right to Work," Lincoln Steffens's exposé of political corruption, "The Shame of Minneapolis," and Ida Tarbell's historical narrative of corporate villainy, "The Oil War of 1872," grew out of three deeply intertwined realities. They were products of a particular historical moment, the genius of the reporters who wrote them, and a new style of journalism that was transforming early-twentieth-century magazines. Each essay tells a compelling tale that resonated with a great many readers in 1903. Each explores problems that remain of great interest to American citizens in this, the last decade of the twentieth century.

Reprinted here together for the first time since their original appearance, the articles are accompanied by the scathing editorial that publisher S. S. McClure ran with them in the January 1903 copy of his magazine. McClure makes it clear that in printing the three essays together he was appealing to the conscience of American citizens. Whether or not their consciences were pricked, readers eagerly scooped up every issue of the magazine. Before long, other periodicals began filling their pages with similar exposés.

The public appetite for stories of criminality, corruption, violence, and evil character requires little explanation for readers in the late twentieth century. Today in "lowbrow" form, tabloid television, daily newspapers, and celebrity gossip magazines provide a steady diet of such fare to huge audiences expanded by revolutionary developments in mass media. "Highbrow" newspapers, magazines, and television programming, too, dig "dirt" by probing beneath the surface of public affairs in a determined effort to provide citizens with the "truth" that many people suspect lurks well beneath the surface of things. Sometimes such reporting results in little more than personal pain and public embarrassment. But very often in the late twentieth century, the consequences have been far-reaching. The mass media have proven to be a potent force in shaping the dynamics of modern American society.

The political influence of writers and reporters depends to a remarkable degree on the convergence of national media, historical moment, and individual artistry. The relative weight each element holds in shaping history cannot be easily discerned. Nonetheless, the recent past offers numerous examples of writers and reporters who left an indelible mark on American history. Consider Michael Harrington's *The Other America*, a heart-wrenching exposé of widespread poverty in a nation of prosperity. When it was published in 1962, the book sent out a clarion call that roused many middle-class Americans from ignorance of these conditions and stirred others from self-satisfied complacency. Harrington's book helped prepare public opinion for the social welfare initiatives that were launched by liberals in the Kennedy years and that were realized, at least in part, by Lyndon Johnson's Great Society programs.

Rachel Carson's brief against pesticides and her plea for renewed human efforts to safeguard our natural resources made her book *Silent Spring* a best-seller in 1962. Carson's book sparked a national debate about environmental issues that remains a vital part of contemporary politics and public policy. Reviled by some and lauded by others, Carson warned Americans of the toxic effects of DDT. In so doing, she helped inspire a new awareness that the fate of the environment is intricately connected to the welfare of human beings. Long after Congress forbade the sale of DDT in 1972, *Silent Spring* was remembered as a book that ushered in fresh American perspectives on ecology.

Last but far from least, the Watergate scandal remains a powerful example of investigative journalism's ability to shape history. Intrepid reporting set in motion a series of events that ultimately stripped Richard Nixon of the presidency in 1974. In this instance, the sleuthing of *Washington Post* reporters Carl Bernstein and Robert Woodward altered the course of American political history.

It would be tempting to see these dramatic examples of mass media's intersection with politics as artifacts of the late twentieth century. In fact, they were anticipated in powerful ways by muckraking journalists in the early part of the century. Before television, before the vast new communications networks that now link our country, before instantaneous news transmission, reporters and editors, writers and politicians were keenly aware of the political power of mass media. Muckraking was not the first example of that awareness, but it remains one of the most compelling for students of American history.

ACKNOWLEDGMENTS

A writer incurs a great many debts, I have discovered, even in the course of preparing a short book. I thank Ernest May, first, for inviting me to participate in his series. Ernest and, at Bedford Books, Chuck Christensen and Sabra Scribner also inspired me with their enthusiasm for the project I proposed. Louise Townsend saw the book through the editorial process and production with just the right amounts of prodding, encouragement, and sympathy. Bedford's managing editor, Elizabeth Schaaf, did an excellent job in overseeing production of the book itself. I am very grateful to Barbara Flanagan for her superb skills as a copyeditor, to Ann Sweeney for her help in clarifying some key concepts in the introduction, and to Richard Keaveny, who facilitated preparation of my manuscript in a great many ways. At Harvard University, Jessica Dorman provided yeoman service as a research assistant throughout the project, locating material and providing excellent suggestions. Deane Lord offered warm encouragement, wise editorial counsel, and her own zesty example as I struggled to understand the world of journalism.

For reading early drafts and providing excellent advice, I both applaud and excuse from any responsibility Alan Brinkley, Allen Davis, Morton Keller, Alexander Keyssar, Jama Lazerow, Theda Skocpol, Bette White, and Susan Williams. Caroline Ford was gracious in permitting me to draw on her knowledge of modern French history. Anne Janowitz proposed fruitful avenues of research and argumentation, punctuated with brilliant observations about the intersection of literature, politics, and history. William Gienapp and Morton Keller were likewise knowledgeable and helpful in clarifying aspects of nineteenth-century politics. Claudia Goldin cheerfully and wisely answered my queries about various aspects of American economic history. Family and friends offered welcome distractions and needed support. Nick Harris and Revan Miles also provided warm reassurance.

My greatest thanks, alas, falls upon deaf ears. To Lincoln Steffens, Ida Tarbell, and Ray Stannard Baker go the enduring gratitude of a sometimes beleaguered historian who profited from seeing the world of turn-of-the-century America through their eyes for a moment and who delighted in the unexpected pleasure of their crisp and vivid prose.

Ellen F. Fitzpatrick

Contents

Late-Nineteenth-Century America and the Origins of Muckraking

The essays reprinted in this volume appeared in the January 1903 edition of *McClure's Magazine* and made it one of the most famous issues of an American magazine ever published. Here—collected in a single place—were three articles, together with an editorial pointing out their significance, that exemplified a kind of investigative journalism relatively new to early-twentieth-century America. This journalism was hard-hitting in tone, often well rooted in fact, and at times brutal in its exposure of venality and corruption. It took as its subject critical social, economic, and political realities in Progressive-era America, the tumultuous age of industrial expansion that spanned the years from roughly 1880 to 1920. Perhaps most important, the new journalism was disseminated nationally in inexpensive magazines that rarely cost more than a nickel or a dime.[1]

Ida Tarbell's "The Oil War of 1872," Lincoln Steffens's "The Shame of Minneapolis," and Ray Stannard Baker's "The Right to Work" were among both the earliest and the best contributions to the new literature of exposure. Like the wider journalism of which they were a part, these essays brought stories from grimy oil fields, seedy gambling dens, and brutal coal mines into the homes of millions of Americans. They added names and faces to the impersonal forces that were redefining the character of American society at the turn of the century. They made fierce conflicts between strangers in distant places appear highly relevant to the concerns of working-class and middle-class Americans, spread across a vast and tremendously diverse land. The journalists' stories had a remarkable immediacy for many Americans who would never be personally affected, in any direct sense, by the gripping and disturbing tales the reporters had to tell.

Theodore Roosevelt called this new investigative journalism "muckraking" in 1906 because he was troubled by its focus and tone. The president likened the journalists to a character in John Bunyan's *Pilgrim's Progress,* the "man with the muckrake," who according to Roosevelt raked up "filth" at his feet and ignored the offer of a "celestial crown." The magazine journalists focused on "evils" in the "body politic," Roosevelt complained, to the extreme of failing to see the good. Although his charge was incited by politics, Roosevelt's characterization of the journalists as "muckrakers" stuck. The work of talented writers and reckless hacks was lumped together from that time forward, obscuring in a haze of charges of sensationalism an important moment in the evolution of twentieth-century American life.[2]

The muckraking years represent a time when the writings of investigative journalists broke through the boundaries of literature and entered the arena of modern politics. They foreshadowed the complex and often contested relationship between journalists and public officials that exists today. In recent American history, the Watergate scandal stands out as perhaps the most dramatic and consequential example of investigative journalism's power to shape national politics. But that power has deep roots in the American past and an especially important precursor in the muckrakers.

The January 1903 issue of *McClure's Magazine* did not mark the advent of muckraking, if we mean by that term the appearance of investigative journalism in magazines. Articles and essays exposing political corruption, business fraud, and labor violence had already appeared in late-nineteenth and early-twentieth-century periodicals. In 1900 McClure himself had published a thinly fictionalized series by Josiah Flynt and Alfred Hodder entitled "True Stories of the Underworld," and he followed it in 1901 with Flynt's shocking account "The World of Graft." Both Lincoln Steffens and Ida Tarbell had published installments of their series on political corruption and Standard Oil, respectively, in the fall of 1902.[3]

Nonetheless, historians widely credit the January 1903 issue of *McClure's* with launching muckraking. By publishing three hard-hitting essays in a single issue and highlighting their message with a provocative editorial, S. S. McClure called attention to a phenomenon and in so doing helped inaugurate a movement. Circulated among approximately 400,000 readers, the January

1903 issue was a fast sell-out. Imitators quickly seized the formula, and countless essays of exposure began to fill the pages of popular magazines. By 1912, more than two thousand such articles had been published. Muckraking had become a nationally recognized part of the American cultural, literary, and political landscape.[4]

This book provides readers with an opportunity to examine the forerunners of modern investigative journalists and to assess the work of three of the best muckrakers. It poses the challenge of seeing how the muckrakers viewed early-twentieth-century American society and how they made sense of the problems they exposed. It allows readers to think about why the muckrakers' writings about big business, political corruption, and labor unrest struck a nerve in the body politic. And perhaps most difficult, it raises the puzzling but important question. How did the writings of the muckrakers actually effect a response to the difficult social, political, and economic problems that prompted their work?

This introduction provides some of the background necessary to analyze the January 1903 issue of *McClure's Magazine*. Through it readers will gain some understanding of the origins of muckraking and the forces that led to the appearance of the magazine itself. Lincoln Steffens, Ida Tarbell, and Ray Stannard Baker, the protagonists of this tale, are introduced here. Also explored are the ways in which the social and historical context of turn-of-the-century America influenced the muckrakers in their choice of subjects and in the substance of their writings. The essay that follows the *McClure's* articles suggests some ways to think about the muckrakers and the significance of their writings for twentieth-century American history.

THE IMPACT OF INDUSTRIALISM

As one reads Lincoln Steffens on political corruption, Ida Tarbell on big business, and Ray Stannard Baker on labor racketeering, it is important to remember that the forces that gave rise to their muckraking essays predated by many years the appearance of *McClure's Magazine*. Indeed, *McClure's* exposés of political corruption, social unrest, civic irresponsibility, and business misdeeds were, in a manner of speaking, old news by 1903. For much of the late nineteenth century, American citizens had engaged in a spirited and sometimes violent debate about the impact of industrialism on their society. The debate took many forms, involved countless participants, produced wildly diverging arguments, provoked deep social conflict, and sparked recurring political discontent. By the turn of the century, the battle over the character and future direction of American society had yielded no clear victory. The turmoil that characterized late-nineteenth-century public life was rooted in powerful historical realities. In fewer than forty years—from 1861 to 1900—the United States experienced a tragic Civil War, severe economic depressions, a massive influx of immigrants, rapid advances in communications, transportation, and technology, an explosion in the size and number of American cities, and an extraordinary expansion of its industrial economy. These changes posed profound challenges to values, institutions, and modes of governance that had taken form in a rural, agrarian society. Among Americans of various classes, they were also the source of considerable anxiety. Immigrants adrift in a new society, workers whose lives were transformed by the harsh conditions and grueling pace of labor in modern factories, farmers unable to gain a hold on the dynamics of agriculture in a boom-and-bust economy, and middle-class Americans keenly aware of the shrinking place of individuals and local communities in a mass society shared a sense of vulnerability.[5]

At the heart of this unrest were three aspects of modern industrialism that would provoke particularly heated debate in the late nineteenth century. By the early twentieth century, they likewise figured prominently in muckraking. The first was the tremendously expanded power and scale of American industrial organizations. Huge corporations that required previously unimagined concentrations of capital and produced colossal fortunes for business owners were, perhaps, the most visible manifestation of industrial capitalism in post–Civil War America. These organizations injected a powerful new force into American politics, society, and economy.

The contrast between these vast business enterprises and most corporations in the pre–Civil War period was a notable feature of the late-nineteenth-century economy. Railroads, with their huge administrative structure, large capital investment, extensive numbers of employees, and complex business activities stood in marked distinction to most American firms in 1861. With thousands of miles of track, hundreds of thousands of employees, and capital accounts reaching into the millions of dollars, large railroad companies foreshadowed new forms of corporate organization that would be the hallmark of the modern American economy.

After the war, vast companies continued to form in manufacturing. By the 1890s, the largest corporations dominated key industries through shrewd new forms of business organization—trusts and holding companies. These new corporate structures enabled manufacturers to combine several firms into a single legal entity with considerable power to control business activity throughout a given industry. During the "great merger movement" at the turn of the century, close to two thousand companies were swallowed up by roughly one hundred fifty giant holding companies. The largest companies routinely controlled more than 40 percent of the market share of their industries. In some sectors of the economy, trusts such as Standard Oil for a time achieved virtual monopolies.

Though keenly aware of the many beneficial changes that vast corporations produced in the United States, many Americans nonetheless greeted their rise with deep suspicion. The Sherman Antitrust Act (1890) reflected Americans' concerns with the impact of huge organizations on the laissez-faire economy. The very existence of these business enterprises raised troubling questions about the roles of individuals, small producers, and local entrepreneurs in a mass industrial society. Weak enforcement by the courts made the Sherman Act itself an example of the persistent conflict over corporate power that was buffeting the polity.[6]

Labor proved to be a second extremely contentious issue in late-nineteenth-century public life. The rise of modern factories changed the structure, pace, and conditions of work for millions of industrial workers. As late as 1910, steelworkers routinely worked twelve-hour days; three-tenths still put in a seven-day week. Well into the 1920s, between fifteen hundred and two thousand men died every year in the nation's coal mines. High industrial accident rates, grueling hours, erratic wages, and persistent unemployment exacted a tremendous toll on the workers whose labor fueled American industrial development.

The pressures on industrial capitalists were of a different order. Unpredictable business cycles, intensive capital requirements, and harsh competition among emerging oligopolies characterized the late-nineteenth-century economy. Among the strategies corporations employed to deal with these realities were various measures that cut labor costs. The result was bitter and often violent confrontations that pitted labor against capital. The 1880s, it has been aptly said, "dripped with blood."[7]

To battle the crushing power of big business, many workers increasingly turned to organization. Banding together into labor unions, they demanded not simply higher wages and shorter hours but, increasingly, recognition of their right to organize and to have their unions represent them in collective bargaining. Many manufacturers fiercely resisted this demand, as did some middle-class Americans who feared the power of organized labor and the violence that seemed to accompany its rise at every turn. Some of the millions of unorganized workers also greeted the trade union movement with a measure of ambivalence. Some agitated for a more inclusive labor movement. Others rejected the mantle of trade unionism, a posture that added an explosive factor to already fierce industrial strikes.[8]

Finally, industrialism fueled intense concerns about the role and responsibilities of government in modern society. Rejecting a tradition of relatively restricted federal power, various groups sought to widen the scope of government to promote their interests within the industrial economy. Some sought a more expansive regulatory state to stabilize and direct laissez-faire capitalism. Others stressed the importance of government intervention to promote the social welfare of diverse groups of needy citizens. Increasingly, however, the granting of government favors to one group clashed with the claims of another as competition between interest groups eroded a sense of the "national good." These conflicts over the distributive and administrative roles of government reached from the local to the federal level.

So too did intense debate over the machinery of democracy and its efficacy. Attacks on the party system, election rules, the organization of municipal government, and rights to the vote were just a few of the issues that divided Americans. Conflict over the rules of politics reflected broader discord about the functions of government. The charges of corruption these disputes inspired were hardly new to late-nineteenth-century American politics. They assumed a new urgency, however, as the spoils of politics grew rich with the expansion of government bureaucracies and as the spoils system was buffeted by ever more intense pressures for reform.

Of particular concern to many Americans was the spread of business influence over politics. Private corporations pursuing public contracts, licenses, and franchises often contributed heavily to and indeed bribed party officials and officeholders to secure lucrative business ventures and favorable terms. At the state level, evidence mounted that powerful business interests were using the considerable sums at their disposal to sway legislators. The growing concentration of economic power among a smaller number of large corporations had similarly profound implications for national politics. Suspicions that the sugar and oil trusts could stave off regulation by lining the pockets of jurists and congressional representatives would soon inflame the rhetoric of politics. In 1890 a revealing cartoon in *Puck* magazine depicted the presidency as a chair being auctioned off to a room full of railroad tycoons and financiers. "None but millionaires need apply: the coming style of Presidential elections" ran its caption. In sum, the vast changes that reshaped the American economy spilled over into American politics. Industrialism increasingly determined the content of late-nineteenth-century politics even as politics alternately accelerated and curtailed the advance of the new industrial society.[9]

Big business, labor, and government thus composed a triangle of interests that informed the debate over the future direction of modern American society. Throughout the 1880s and 1890s, the American political landscape was dotted with reform movements that sought to correct the "evils" of industrialism. "Men struggled," Tarbell later reflected, "to get at causes, to find corrections, to humanize and socialize the country, for then as now there were those who dreamed of a good world although at times it seemed to them to be going mad."

Clearly there was no shortage of problems to be addressed or absence of voices clamoring for change. Yet the forms political agitation took were varied. They ranged from the formation of ambitious new political parties to the creation of countless voluntary organizations to political assassination and the tossing of anarchist bombs. Accompanying, and even at times inspiring, these various tactics was an extraordinarily rich literature of social criticism that quickly became a force in public life. These writings form an important backdrop for muckraking.[10]

Among the early examples of social analysis that fueled political activism was the work of lay economist and reformer Henry George. His *Poverty and Progress* (1879) stressed the role of rising land values in shaping social and economic inequality. George's analysis and his advocacy of a "single tax" on land struck a chord among many in his vast readership. In the 1880s and 1890s a national social movement of "single taxers" transformed George's brief for economic reform into a surprisingly popular crusade. Edward Bellamy's wildly popular utopian novel *Looking Backward* (1888) portrayed the United States in the year 2000 under a system that resembled state socialism. The book sparked a similar wave of reform enthusiasm. Ironically, industrialism itself had created new opportunities for writers and intellectuals to advance their critical views. Technological advances in printing as well as nationalized communications networks helped carry the writings of social critics, political agitators, and intellectuals to ever larger and more diverse audiences.

Virtually all of the issues that informed muckraking surfaced, at least in broad terms, in the late-nineteenth-century critique of industrialism. Newspaper editor Henry Demarest Lloyd took on the unsavory business dealings and scandal-ridden history of the Standard Oil Company in *Wealth against Commonwealth* (1894), nearly a decade before Ida Tarbell's muckraking exposés appeared in *McClure's Magazine*. Urban political corruption, the disgraceful deal making between dirty politicians and greedy businessmen was fodder for political cartoonists such as Thomas Nast and mugwump* essayists such as E. L. Godkin twenty years before Lincoln Steffens raked up this muck in the pages of *McClure's*. Labor unrest and the presumed perils of trade unionism inspired much critical writing in the late nineteenth century. In Bellamy's utopia, labor conflict had ceased to exist in the year 2000, but so had the trade unionist. Long before Ray Stannard Baker cast a critical eye on labor racketeering, the dangers of the labor movement had been intimated by writers, novelists, and essayists.[11]

By the 1890s, American fiction seemed especially responsive to the social

---

*The mugwumps were independent Republicans who bolted from their party in 1884 to support Democratic reform governor of New York Grover Cleveland for the presidency. They criticized the party system and agitated for good government and "morality in politics." Newspaper writers were highly visible in the movement. (Keller, *Affairs of State,* 550–52.)

unrest of late-nineteenth-century society. In novels such as Stephen Crane's
Maggie: A Girl of the Streets (1893) and Theodore Dreiser's *Sister Carrie* (1900),
cities emerged as dark and forbidding places full of evils poorly anticipated
by the young women victimized there. Frank Norris in *The Octopus* (1901)
exposed the cutthroat tactics of America's first corporate titans—the railroads—against farmers. He followed that novel with a tale of the manipulation
of farmers by wheat brokers in *The Pit* (1902). Hamlin Garland offered a
devastating portrait of rural life in *Main Traveled Roads* (1891). As early as
1873, Mark Twain aptly characterized the corruption of democracy in *The
Gilded Age*. These fictional accounts expressed well the apprehensions
aroused by the new industrial society.

So, too, did the burgeoning research efforts of American social scientists
to chart the impact of immigration, industrialization, and urbanization on
modern society. Employing new empirical methods, including social surveys
of urban communities, academics found in the turmoil of late-nineteenth-
century America a laboratory for their research and a rationale for their
professional ambitions. Settlement houses and voluntary associations also
mounted social investigations in an effort to better serve their constituencies.
Indeed, reformers and academics often found common ground in their belief
that scientific knowledge provided the best hope for solving conflicts that
divided workers from capitalists, immigrants from native-born Americans,
those who wished for expansive social welfare measures from those who
rejected a more activist government. This faith in investigation, fact finding,
and objectivity deeply informed late-nineteenth-century intellectual life. It
would likewise be reflected in muckraking.[12]

In sum, the problems that inspired muckraking were not entirely new to
the early twentieth century. Americans were hardly unaware of and unmoved
by the momentous changes that were transforming their society. Nor was a
critical stance toward industrialism lacking among writers, essayists, popular agitators, and intellectuals. What, then, was new about muckraking?
To answer this question, it is important to focus closely on changes in
the character of journalism, the production of news, and the rise of mass-
circulation magazines.

THE "MAGAZINE REVOLUTION"

Muckraking owed its beginnings, in part, to late-nineteenth-century innova-
tions in the way news and literature were produced and disseminated. Newspapers and magazines had been available throughout the nineteenth century,

but magazines of good quality were expensive before the mid-1880s, with periodicals such as *Harper's Weekly* and *Century* selling for the then princely sum of thirty-five cents. Their price tended to restrict their circulation to better educated and more affluent readers. The contents of these magazines were often literary. Though some journals printed essays that addressed pressing public issues, their perspective frequently reflected the conservative politics of the editors and their presumed readership. Critics of political corruption, for example, were often as disdainful of the immigrants the bosses served as they were of the spoils system. Peering down at the masses through lenses tinted with erudition and gentility, the editors and writers of many late-nineteenth-century magazines showed no genuine sympathy for or particular interest in the concerns of working people.[13]

Newspapers, however, reached out to a broader base in their efforts to gratify readers. Before the Civil War, working men and women could follow crime stories and political high jinks through the medium of the "penny press." The close ties between many antebellum newspapers and the political parties made them frankly partisan and a source of popularity. But it was the post–Civil War period that brought newspapers their great expansion in numbers and circulation. As they became increasingly free from the restraints imposed on them by their ties to political parties, newspapers of all kinds began to reflect the professionalization of journalism in the late nineteenth century. The greater stress on independence and objectivity heightened the power of and, its seems, the public appetite for political and urban news.

Thus, long before muckraking ever began, the press made a place in American life for crime stories, politics, and all the other bits of urban desiderata that made up the daily news. Newspapers were nonetheless inhibited by their format from presenting extensive and in-depth essays that probed current social issues in a thoughtful manner. They had large audiences but lacked the depth of coverage a magazine format could potentially provide. Magazines, however, often lacked a mass audience, an attention to human-interest stories, and the political sympathies that would appeal to a broad readership.

Technological developments in the 1880s allowed magazines to become more like newspapers both in content and in garnering a wide readership. The price of paper dropped sharply as wood supplanted cloth in paper manufacture and economic downturns further depressed paper and production costs. The inauguration of halftone photoengraving as a process for reproducing photographs offered an alternative to the time-consuming, costly, and cumbersome woodcuts that provided magazines with one of their most appealing features—illustrations. Although news photographs dated back to the 1840s, until the 1880s they could not be reproduced with type by the presses used to print newspapers and magazines. Instead, photographs provided models for artists, who prepared illustrations from them and then turned their drawings over for wood engraving. Even when the halftone process made it possible to use news photography, some editors resisted. By the late 1890s speed presses made halftones increasingly available to newspapers and magazines.

These technical advances in printing and photography soon enabled magazines to compete more aggressively with newspapers as sources of timely information and lively news. Even with the advent of Sunday magazine supplements, newspapers often still faced space and geographical restrictions that did not encumber magazines. Some of the best-established and most respected magazines responded slowly to the advantages technology placed before them. Others began to cut their prices. Entirely new, cheaper magazines also began to appear, supported in part by expanding advertising revenue. The titles of these magazines—*Everybody's, Cosmopolitan*—revealed their bid for diverse, mass readership.[14]

One of the most daring, and soon to be most successful, of the new illustrated monthlies was *McClure's Magazine.* Launched in June 1893 at fifteen cents a copy, *McClure's* immediately set off a price war that drove down the cost of several major journals. In the summer of 1895, *McClure's* dropped its price to ten cents a copy to compete with *Munsey's* and *Cosmopolitan.* A new era in magazine publishing was thereby ushered in. The price war now placed magazines in an excellent position to compete with newspapers for advertising revenue.[15]

The advent of inexpensive, well-produced, mass-circulation magazines proved decisive to muckraking. For the first time Americans of diverse social classes had a consistently produced and nationally distributed source of information, entertainment, and news. The class matrix of periodical readers broadened with the advent of cheap mass-circulation magazines. Millions of Americans purchased the new magazines; skyrocketing circulation figures alone suggest that turn-of-the-century magazines tapped an expanding and increasingly diverse readership. Rising literacy rates also widened the potential market for magazines (although presumably some subscribers could not read and simply thumbed through their copies in search of photographs). Still, middle-class Americans with change to spend on reading material and enough schooling to profit from several long pages of narrative no doubt made up the bulk of readership.

However deep within the American social strata cut their readership, the mass-circulation magazines reached wide across the nation in their subscription lists. As was true of so many elements of modern life, the rise of the new magazines provided for a more integrated national cultural experience. For good or ill, readers in great cities and small towns, on farms and in factories, in the Northeast and across the Great Plains could—on a monthly basis—read the same essays, short stories, and bits of news. This was a development of major importance not just for American culture but for American politics.[16]

The photographs and illustrations that studded the magazines were also freighted with cultural and political significance. As early as 1888, a New York newspaper had run drawings with the tag "Flashes from the Slums" that were based on the photographs of police reporter Jacob Riis. Riis recognized that visual images could make a deep impression on observers, striking reservoirs of feeling that no amount of narrative description could ever reach. When Riis's brutal exposé of conditions in New York's immigrant-filled tenements, *How the Other Half Lives,* was published in 1890, the book contained a handful of halftones. These extraordinary photographs provided dramatic and poignant evidence of the misery that had incited Riis. Curiosity, fear, and a wish to literally see the face of industrial society drew Americans to the new illustrated magazines. Photographs of human beings seemed to war against growing fears that individuals mattered little in a mass industrial society. Muckraking would exploit these concerns by making liberal use of head shots of famous personalities and news photography.[17]

Still, the mere existence of illustrated, inexpensive mass circulation magazines does not account for the emergence of a literature of exposure. That depended in much larger part on the skills of a new generation of professional reporters who brought unusual experiences and perspectives to bear on American society. Of central importance in shaping *McClure's Magazine* was the editorial staff gathered by the journal's founders, Samuel Sidney (S. S.) McClure and John Phillips.

Former classmates at Knox College in Illinois, McClure and Phillips had come to magazine publishing as syndicators of fiction, critical essays, and photographs for use in newspapers and magazines. A man of terrific energy and sometimes wild imagination, McClure spearheaded the syndicating business. In a typical mood of restlessness, he dreamed up the notion of starting his own magazine. While Phillips provided the decisive initial funding, it was McClure who recruited much of the editorial and writing talent. He used his extensive contacts with writers, essayists, and publishers to enlist outstanding literary talent for his magazine.

Early issues of *McClure's* offered an admirable mix of fiction from authors such as Rudyard Kipling, Robert Louis Stevenson, and O. Henry, essays on science and inventions, including profiles of Thomas Edison and Alexander Graham Bell, and adventure stories featuring exotic places and wild animals. But it was S. S. McClure's success in hiring a group of well-educated, ambitious, and well-traveled young reporters that proved decisive to the development of muckraking. An exploration of the personal, social, and historical forces that led these young reporters to *McClure's* provides further important clues to the origins of muckraking.[18]

THE MAKING OF THE JOURNALISTS

One of S. S. McClure's greatest and earliest finds was Ida Minerva Tarbell, a woman who would put *McClure's Magazine* on the map and, later, help establish its reputation for muckraking. Born in 1857 and raised in the booming oil towns of northwestern Pennsylvania, Tarbell as a child witnessed the ravages and glories that marked the early days of petroleum production in the United States. She was just shy of three years old when her father brought his young family to Oil Creek, drawn by Edwin L. Drake's discovery of oil in Titusville in 1859. In spite of her young age, Ida remembered to the end of her life gruesome scenes of accidental death and physical destruction all too common in the oil regions. When the first gushers shot up from the ground, the properties of oil were poorly understood. Few producers foresaw oil's tremendous future as an energy resource and boundless source of capital; fewer still appreciated the dangers associated with drilling and refining petroleum.[19]

Ghastly fires and explosions claimed lives in terrible accidents, such as the one that occurred when a woman "hurrying to build a fire in her cookstove poured oil on the wood before she had made sure there were no live coals in the firebox.... An awful explosion occurred," Tarbell recalled, and the woman and "two neighbors who ran to her assistance were burned to a crisp." The sight of their bodies terrified the seven-year-old Tarbell, who defied parental instructions to stay away from the home where the corpses were laid out.[20]

The physical damage wreaked upon a once verdant landscape also remained vivid in Tarbell's remembrance of her early years. She had spent the first three years of her life on her grandparents' farm in rural Pennsylvania, a lush setting that contrasted sharply with the harshness of her new life at Oil Creek. Remembering her childhood on "the edge of an active oil farm and oil town," Tarbell wrote in her eighties that

> no industry of man in its early days has ever been more destructive of beauty, order, decency, than the production of petroleum.... All about us rose derricks, squatted enginehouses and tanks; the earth about them was streaked and damp with the dumpings of pumps, which brought up regularly the sand and clay and rock through which the drill had made its way. If oil was found, if the well flowed, every tree, every shrub, every bit of grass in the vicinity was coated with black grease and left to die. Tar and oil stained everything. If the well was dry a rickety derrick, piles of debris, oily holes were left, for nobody ever cleaned up in those days.

These early impressions and experiences would lend an extraordinary vividness and passion to Tarbell's writings on the history of Standard Oil.[21]

The Tarbells were also beneficiaries of the boom in the petroleum industry, a fact that would shape Ida's future investigative work. Her father recognized the profits that might accrue to a joiner capable of building wooden tanks for oil storage. He started a business that took advantage of this need, quickly turning a handsome profit and advancing the social and material standing of his growing family. Investment in the oil business followed, as did a large and stately new home for the Tarbell family in Cherry Run, Pennsylvania. As soon as her father "had more money than the actual needs of the family required," he began buying books and subscribing to magazines. Ida had her first exposure to great literature in *Harper's Monthly*. Purloined copies of the *Police Gazette* gave hints of urban crimes, shady characters, sins of "wantonness and wickedness." Tarbell's worldview was itself shaped by the growing popularity of American magazines.[22]

Her parents' comfortable economic circumstances and their belief in women's rights to educational opportunities enabled Ida Tarbell to become a member of the first generation of college-educated women in the United States. The only woman in her freshman class at Allegheny College, Tarbell immersed herself in the study of science. She graduated in 1880, taught school in Ohio for two years, and when that career failed to hold her interest, accepted a position with a monthly magazine edited by an acquaintance of the Tarbell family.[23]

The Chautauquan launched Tarbell's career as a journalist. This magazine had it origins in the popular Chautauqua movement, a religiously inspired initiative to spread education and learning to adults by means of summer institutes and home instruction. *The Chautauquan* supplemented the program of home instruction with timely articles about current social issues as well as literary and science essays. It offered Tarbell the opportunity to learn the ins and outs of preparing a magazine, from proofreading to setting type to writing and researching stories for an audience of men and women pursuing their education at home. In the summer, when the magazine suspended publication, Tarbell worked on the Chautauqua daily newspaper that took its place. As a writer for these periodicals, Tarbell immersed herself in the turbulent social and political conflicts of the 1880s. *The Chautauquan* supported many reform issues of the day, including the eight-hour day, the Knights of Labor (the great labor union of the 1870s and 1880s), temperance, antimonopoly crusades, and housing reform.[24]

A developing interest in social issues and, particularly, in the role of women in public life increasingly influenced Tarbell's work. Fascinated by the role of women in the French Revolution, she decided to travel to France to research and write a biography of Madame Roland, a fiery Republican who went to the guillotine with the famous cry "O Liberty! What crimes are committed in thy name!" In Paris, Tarbell began for the first time to envisage a career in journalism, realizing that she might support herself by freelance writing for American newspapers and magazines. That decision, unorthodox for a woman of Tarbell's generation, reflected a firm grasp of the media explosion in the United States and the working of syndicates that would make possible a professional writing career. It also revealed a consciousness that comparative studies of European societies could bring into sharper relief the American national experience.

Tarbell enjoyed quick success as a freelance journalist. From her small but enviably situated rooms in the Latin Quarter, she ventured into the streets of Paris in the summer of 1891. She wrote stories for American newspapers designed to offer a comparative perspective on the "great agitation over the condition and the conduct of American cities." These projects competed for time with work on her biography of Madame Roland. At the Sorbonne, Tarbell enriched her understanding of her subject's world by taking classes in French history, literature, and political economy.[25]

Her forays around Paris to gather material for her biography of Madame Roland led Tarbell into the salons of French socialist intellectuals. Invited to a weekly dinner followed by discussion at the home of Sorbonne historian Charles Siegnobos, Tarbell listened to impassioned debates about the state and future of the French Republic. Though her study of Roland left her skeptical about revolutionary means and ends, she admired the fierce intelligence of the French scholars and their passionate commitment to social and political change. The political turbulence in France gave a sharp edge to Tarbell's musing about revolution. She began to see revolution as the product of forces that built incrementally, only to be loosened by men and women who were then powerless to control the surge of change. These conclusions disappointed Tarbell, who wanted to place her faith in human agency. Yet they gave her a richer sense of the complexity of history and a keen intuitive feeling for the importance of social and political forces in shaping a nation's experience.[26]

The knowledge of France that Tarbell gained from her studies and her associations also strengthened her stock in the literary marketplace. She sold her first story to *Scribner's* by crafting a tale designed to capitalize on the magazine's taste for French culture. She sold other short pieces on Parisian life to S. S. McClure's syndicate. McClure was intrigued by the productive female expatriate and made arrangements for further contributions. In 1894, when Tarbell returned home, McClure hired her to write an essay on Napoleon's life to accompany a series of portraits reprinted in his recently launched magazine. The story exemplified one of the most appealing features in *McClure's:*

character sketches of individuals lavishly illustrated with portraits. Late-nineteenth-century readers were much drawn to these "Human Documents," as they were called, which made use of advances in photography and printing to offer rarely glimpsed visual representations of famous personalities.[27]

Tarbell's series on Napoleon proved so successful that McClure quickly proposed that she prepare a series of essays on the life of Abraham Lincoln. The Civil War remained a compelling theme in American life and letters in the 1890s, and for many citizens Lincoln was a vivid memory. Tarbell's first essay on Lincoln, "The Early Life of Lincoln," published in November 1895, nearly doubled the magazine's circulation. Within three months of its appearance, *McClure's* had added 140,000 subscribers to its rolls. During the fall of 1894, circulation of the magazine had stood at approximately 60,000; by 1896 it skyrocketed to nearly 260,000. By that time, Tarbell had joined the *McClure's* staff as a contributing editor. She spent four years researching and writing further essays on Lincoln, an assignment that preoccupied her until the outbreak of the Spanish-American War in 1898.[28]

The war, as Tarbell herself noted, marked a turning point for *McClure's Magazine,* its writers, editors, and readership. Inflamed in part by newspaper accounts of Spanish atrocities against Cuban civilians and the sinking of the American battleship *Maine* in Havana harbor, the public developed a voracious appetite for war news. Live-action photographs and extensive reporting of the progress of the war, including eyewitness accounts, sent *McClure's* circulation through the roof. The magazine itself seemed poised, as the title of one series ran, on "The Edge of the Future." Indeed, more than any other single factor, it was the war that plunged *McClure's* into public life. The magazine suddenly became an important source of news for Americans eager to follow the progress of the fighting. The convergence of a fast-breaking news event of national importance, a burgeoning list of subscribers impatient for war news, and a format that could outdo newspapers in depth, if not timeliness, of coverage created extraordinary opportunities for magazines. McClure exploited these opportunities by mustering the best journalistic talent he could find. At the moment of the war, he turned to experienced newspaper reporters and came up with Ray Stannard Baker, who was offered a position as a contributing editor for *McClure's*.[29]

Baker's early life and career resembled Tarbell's in some important ways. Born in 1870, Baker was thirteen years younger than Tarbell. But like his female colleague, he belonged to the generation of Americans who came of age in the post–Civil War years. The son of a Wisconsin businessman, Baker too grew up with many advantages. And like Tarbell, he remembered his childhood home as a "house of books"; he especially treasured youthful magazines such as *Harper's Young People* and *St. Nicholas Magazine.* As a male, Baker made a more likely collegian than Tarbell. Still, in this period he was privileged in his ability to pursue a higher education. After sampling science, agriculture, and literature at Michigan Agricultural College, Baker began to think in terms of a legal career. But those plans were quickly abandoned within weeks of beginning law school at the University of Michigan in 1892. Course work in literature and a seminar in "rapid writing," a precursor to journalism courses, revealed previously unseen horizons. Baker left the University of Michigan after one term and found a job as a newspaper reporter for the *Chicago Record*. It was the start of a literary career.[30]

Few American cities better exemplified the ills and the possibilities of the new industrial society than did Chicago in the 1890s. Amid the grandeur of the World's Fair was the squalor of a city that had grown fast and big, rich in its burgeoning industries, poor in the provisions made for a huge, diverse, and sometimes desperate working class. Shortly after Baker's arrival, the Depression of 1893 brought "unprecedented extremes of poverty, unemployment, unrest. . . . Every day during that bitter winter," Baker recalled, "the crowds of ragged, shivering, hopeless human beings in Chicago seemed to increase." Drawn to this spectacle of misery, Baker walked the city and gathered stories for his newspaper.

> I reported the establishment of huge soup kitchens where I watched the long lines of the miserable unemployed waiting to be fed. Sometimes I talked with a man here and there, and often visited the police stations and "flop-houses" where they spent the winter nights. I attended the mass meetings called by citizens to deal with the crisis. I watched what the labor unions, the churches, and the social settlements were trying to do. I listened to the fiery prophecies of the soap-box orators on the Lake Front. Each of them had his own devil, each his own utopia. I wrote three or four times as much every day as the *Record* could or would publish.[31]

No setting could have better prepared Baker for his future efforts as a muckraker.

In Chicago Baker watched history in the making and reported what he saw with a mixture of awe and ambivalence. He marched with Coxey's Army to Washington, D.C., in 1894, following with fascination the several hundred unemployed men mobilized by Populist leader Jacob S. Coxey who traveled by foot from Ohio to the nation's capital demanding economic relief. The depression of 1893 created widespread unemployment—as many as a million laborers idle—and pervasive (and realistic) fears about the prospects of economic recovery. One day's critical report of the "unemployed tramps" who demanded a government public works program and an improbable increase in circulating currency offset Baker's praise on another day for the "miracle" of the "petition in boots" that represented "a manifestation of the prevailing unrest and dissatisfaction among the laboring classes."

Within three days of finishing his story on Coxey's Army, Baker was asked to cover the Pullman strike. The strike began when George Pullman responded to depressed economic conditions by dismissing a third of his workers at the Pullman Palace Car Company and reducing by 30 percent the wages of those he decided to keep. Rents in Pullman, the company town he built near Chicago for his employees, were not, however, similarly reduced. A walkout ensued. Pullman's refusal to negotiate prompted the American Railway Union to call a strike against trains that used Pullman cars. The strike snarled railroad transportation, prompted federal intervention, the calling out of federal troops, and the arrest and imprisonment of ARU leader Eugene V. Debs. Faced with "one of the greatest industrial conflicts in the history of the country," Baker threw his sympathy behind the workers and Debs's American Railway Union. Much taken with Debs, whom he intervened in a Cook County jail cell, Baker nonetheless disliked the violence of the strike and doubted whether "such anarchy" could be "permitted in a civilized society."[32]

Baker's views about such matters did not dull the exceptional power and clarity of his reporting. He struggled to report "the facts" as baldly as he could. Yet Baker also captured the human face that appeared in the midst of poverty and labor violence. To do so was to master an art that appealed greatly to his audience, increasingly propelled in their everyday lives by impersonal forces and powerfully drawn in their literary tastes to the luminescence of human personalities. "I learned," Baker later explained, "that common human suffering and common human joy, if truly reported, never grow stale."[33]

Baker seemed equally sensitive to another mood of the day. Assigned to follow English journalist and reformer William T. Stead's campaign to uplift Chicago, the cub reporter felt the "new and powerful impulse in social criticism" proffered by an emerging "new journalism." Baker's interests focused on the "new problems" of unemployment and conflict between labor and capital. Yet he was simultaneously drawn to fiction writing and tried valiantly, often successfully, to find a place for his stories in the magazines.[34]

Inspired by Ida Tarbell's successful series on Lincoln, Baker submitted to *McClure's* an account of his uncle's role in capturing President Lincoln's assassin, John Wilkes Booth. This was reaching for the top, as *McClure's,* Baker noted, "was then the sensation of the publishing world." The acceptance letter came from Ida Tarbell, and thus began not only "a life-long friendship" between the two reporters but Baker's new relationship with *McClure's.* Invited to come east to meet the editors, he made his first trip to New York in 1897.

The prospect of writing regularly for *McClure's* thrilled Baker, as did promised fees and future royalties. As a new father, Baker found himself so pressed for cash he could not help but see his new infant as a weighty financial responsibility. "Our baby herself, who was blue-eyed and fat and happy—altogether quite satisfactory—" he later remembered, "had cost me, at lowest calculation, about seventy thousand words, a small volume like Emerson's essays. All the various unnameable fixings that went with a baby I put down at ten thousand words, the equivalent of two or three substantial short stories." These concerns prompted Baker to seize the opportunity when McClure offered a regular staff position in January 1898.[35]

Arriving just days after the sinking of the *Maine,* Baker was soon assigned to cover the Spanish-American War. Many years later he somberly reflected that the conflict marked the moment when "America as a nation began . . . to awaken suddenly to a sense of a swiftly expanding world." At the time, Baker's pieces on Roosevelt and his Rough Riders (a regiment of U.S. Cavalry volunteers), the reconstruction of Cuba, and the naval battles largely celebrated the war.

When the war was over, Baker had the opportunity to enrich his growing sense of internationalism by reporting from Germany about the march of science and industry there. His travels in Europe gave him an unusually cosmopolitan outlook on American society, another attribute he shared with his colleague Ida Tarbell. Upon his return, Baker wrote a few largely celebratory pieces for *McClure's* on the newly emergent trusts, including an admiring portrait of U.S. Steel and a detailed analysis of the Northern Securities Company, a giant railroad combination. But by the winter of 1900 Baker had become literally sick and tired from his travels and his work for the magazine. John Phillips did not want to see his talented writer go and offered him the generous terms of a leave of absence with salary, which Baker gratefully accepted. When he left *McClure's* his departure made a place for Lincoln Steffens at the magazine, although it was understood that Baker would continue to contribute to *McClure's.*[36]

The employment of Steffens completed the triumvirate that would soon make *McClure's* the leading muckraking magazine. Tarbell considered Steffens "the most brilliant addition to the *McClure's* staff in my time." Certainly Steffens brought a forceful personality, unusual abilities, and youthful experiences made possible by family privilege.

"I was well born," Steffens once wrote, aptly describing his origins. Born in April 1866, just a few days shy of the first anniversary of Lincoln's death, Steffens received a name from his father that reflected the older man's admiration and mourning for the slain president. Steffens's father, a successful businessman like Tarbell's and Baker's fathers, had migrated from Illinois to California in the 1860s. His mother, an Englishwoman who deeply regretted her lack of education, raised her only son and her three daughters to value schooling above material things. This emphasis led to college educations for all the Steffens children, daughters and son alike.

The Steffens family lived in style in Sacramento, inhabiting a much admired Victorian home that later became the governor's mansion for the state of California. Steffens spent his boyhood on horseback, devoting long hours to exploring the Sacramento Valley. An easily distracted child and rebellious adolescent, Steffens was sent away to boarding school in San Mateo at age sixteen. There he displayed an early aptitude for writing and literature and an enthusiasm for military science. He continued his pursuits in all these areas as an undergraduate at the University of California at Berkeley between 1885 and 1889.[37]

Steffens's academic experience at Berkeley gave him a low opinion of American college life. "It is possible," he later argued, "to get an education at a university. It has been done; not often." He once proposed a series for a magazine to be entitled "Is There Any Intellectual Life in Our Colleges?" The question was inspired by his years at Berkeley. Preoccupied with parties, quail hunting, fraternity life, sports, college pranks, and beer drinking, Steffens was a poor student. But in spite of undistinguished grades, he had a deep intellectual curiosity and when he pursued study on his own he enjoyed history, literature, philosophy, and political economy. At the close of senior year, having "worked, sacrificed my interests," and on occasion "cheated" to win his "worthless baccalaureate," he decided to continue his education in Germany, ironically enough to study ethics.[38]

Steffens followed a path well traveled by young American graduate students when he chose to enroll at the University of Berlin in 1889. German universities set the standard for graduate education in the late nineteenth century when professionalization in the United States began to take hold. Steffens attended lectures in art history, ethics, and economics at Berlin and then traveled to Heidelberg to study Hegelian philosophy. He was searching to find a scientific basis for ethics. Philosophers, Steffens soon concluded, could not provide one. So he left Heidelberg for Leipzig in the hopes of finding answers from the experimental psychologist Wilhelm Max Wundt.

Instead of illumination Steffens found sheer intellectual torture in Wundt's laboratory. "The laboratory where we sought the facts," he later recalled, "and measured them by machinery was a graveyard where the old idealism walked as a dreadful ghost and philosophical thinking was a sin." Though Steffens valued the training in empirical science that he received at Leipzig, he found no ethics in experimental psychology. By the spring of 1891 Steffens knew his quest had reached a dead end. The only inspiration he felt was "to go and make love myself to a pretty American girl who sat just behind me in Wundt's lectures. It was unethical, but I did it," he remembered. The romance led to Steffens's marriage in the fall of 1891.[39]

By that time, Steffens had moved on to still another European city and university. This time it was Paris and the Sorbonne, where Ida Tarbell was also then studying. Steffens dabbled further in psychology, wrote fiction, and continued to ruminate about ethics. At long last, his father's patience with Steffens's wanderlust ran out. Joseph Steffens sent his son word that it was time to come home. When Steffens arrived in New York in 1892, he received a note his father had left for him that quickly sobered the young man up. "Enclosed please find one hundred dollars, which should keep you till you can find a job and support yourself."[40]

Writing had been the one constant in Steffens's haphazard intellectual life, and so he finally turned to journalism when forced to make a living. Family connections landed him a job at the New York *Evening Post,* a conservative newspaper edited by E. L. Godkin, the founding editor of *The Nation.* At first, Steffens's beat was Wall Street. During the depression of 1893, he witnessed what he cynically described as "the joy of a panic" that made money for some brokers while the "public" suffered. Covering Wall Street and its environs, he became acutely aware of the strong and often unsavory connections that linked the world of late-nineteenth-century business to the dynamics of American politics.[41]

Assignments to metropolitan financial and political stories and anticorruption campaigns against the police followed. While reporting on the state legislature's Lexow Commission investigations into police corruption in 1894, Steffens began to develop a somewhat paradoxical view of good and evil in city politics. He admired the "Samsons" among the grafters—essentially honest men who had been drawn into corruption by the system, confessed their wrongs, and ultimately used their knowledge of the system to help dismantle it. But he also observed with pessimism the political reformers who lacked not only an understanding of the spoils system but also the strength of character and courage of their convictions to actually effect real change. Steffens later explained, "I saw enough of it to realize that reform politics was still politics, only worse; reformers were not so smooth as professional politicians, and it seemed to me they were not so honest—which was a very confusing theory to me."[42]

As he covered the ground of municipal politics, Steffens began to penetrate the dens of urban political thievery that would become the central focus of *The Shame of the Cities,* the 1904 book that collected his *McClure's* articles on urban political corruption. Instructed to cover activities at police headquarters, Steffens got himself a thorough education in the working of the Tammany organization. Tammany was a Democratic political machine* that exerted an often controlling influence on late-nineteenth and early-twentieth-century New York City politics. Led by a succession of powerful and notorious "bosses," Tammany earned a reputation for both corruption and extraordinary political acumen. The Tammany beat exposed Steffens to the complex influence dealing that pervaded urban politics. In New York City, he learned, there was a close association between criminals, the police, and the machine.[43]

His work for the *Evening Post* also brought Steffens into contact with two men who, by their example, suggested ways of addressing the corruption endemic in the city. Veteran police reporter Jacob Riis did more than simply report the all too routine suicides, fires, and murders in the city's neighborhoods. Steffens observed:

> These were the stories which all the reporters got; only Riis wrote them as stories, with heart, humor, and understanding. And having "seen" the human side of the crime or the disaster, he had taken note also of the house or the block of the street where it happened. He went back and described that, too; he called on the officers and landlords who permitted the conditions, and "blackmailed" them into reforms.

Riis's ability to see beyond the immediate story to grasp the bigger news made a greater impression on Steffens than did his crusading reform zeal. Traversing the often treacherous alleys of Mulberry Street, Steffens began to observe with a more seeing eye the city's "demiworld." Later, as a newspaper editor himself, Steffens would speak of his preference for the "fresh-staring eyes" of a cub reporter over "the informed mind and blunted pencil" of a seasoned but unfeeling journalist. Coverage of the Lexow Commission hearings led Steffens to Theodore Roosevelt. His association with Roosevelt would in turn lead Steffens to *McClure's*.[44]

Appointed police commissioner by New York's reform Mayor William L. Strong, Roosevelt struck Steffens as a man of quick intelligence and terrific energy. At first, Steffens found in Roosevelt reason to believe in the possibilities of reform politics. He would later conclude that Roosevelt "was an honest man; he could not tell a lie until he had made himself believe it." But in these early years Steffens responded strongly to TR's magnetic personality and his crusading spirit. When Steffens moved on from the *Evening Post* in 1897 to accept a job at the *Commercial Advertiser,* he continued to follow Roosevelt's exploits. Seeing in TR's Rough Rider days superb copy for his magazine, S. S. McClure approached Steffens for a series of articles on Roosevelt. The first essay appeared in May 1899, and with its success Steffens began to figure

*Political machines were political organizations designed to keep a particular party or faction in office.

more prominently in the thinking of McClure. When the magazine's staff was depleted by unexpected departures in 1900, Steffens was offered the job of managing editor.[45]

Steffens wanted to bring more news into the magazine. Stories that "ran long" in the newspapers lost punch with the newspaper readership. Space restrictions impeded depth of analysis. Steffens envisioned a monthly magazine that "could come along, tell the whole, completed story all over again, and bring out the meaning of it all with comment." His notions suited the ambitions of *McClure's,* and he joined the magazine in 1901. His arrival completed the staff that would decisively launch muckraking. Describing his feeling on joining *McClure's,* Steffens later wrote: "It was just like springing up from a bed and diving into the lake—and life. The water was cold."[46]

Ida Tarbell, Ray Stannard Baker, and Lincoln Steffens brought the experience, skill, energy, and insight of their generation to *McClure's Magazine.* They came of age at a moment when Americans were struggling to absorb the realities of the new industrial society. They assumed the burden of that struggle themselves as soon as they began to work as journalists—in the midst of the depression of 1893. Higher education had exposed them to a much changed intellectual world shaped by the rise of modern science, entranced by the power of scientific fact, and moved by professionalization to value objectivity. As privileged young men and women, the reporters were also stunned by the human suffering they observed firsthand. Searching for copy, they walked the streets of the cities, came face to face with the poor, attended the meetings of radicals and reformers, and struggled to find the larger meaning behind the heartache they saw. The reporters had literary pretensions. They cared about writing and they wanted to do it well. Finally, they found a lucrative venue for their stories and a supportive backer for their intellectual and professional ambitions in S. S. McClure's magazine.[47]

Three factors converged at the turn of the century, then, to support the emergence of muckraking in the magazines. The first was a climate of social upheaval, social criticism, and reform inspired by the American experience with industrialism. This climate did much to determine the content of muckraking. Second, the appearance of national mass-circulation magazines offered a forum for essays and articles on the pressing issues of the day. These magazines made it possible for muckraking to become a powerful influence on public opinion. Finally, a young generation of professional reporters was able to bring together the moment and the magazines in an extraordinary way. They provided the muscle and much of the brain power for muckraking. The convergence of historical moment, institutional support, generational preoccupations, and individual imagination, skill, and experience set the stage for muckraking.

FINDING THE STORY: THE GENESIS OF THE MUCKRAKERS' INVESTIGATIVE REPORTING

Before turning to the muckraking essays in the January 1903 issue of *McClure's Magazine,* readers may find it useful to know how Steffens, Tarbell, and Baker happened upon their stories and went about investigating the conditions that informed their accounts. In his accompanying editorial, S. S. McClure stressed that the appearance of the three muckraking essays in a single issue of the magazine was a "coincidence." This claim was rather disingenuous. The editor himself had a strong hand in directing his reporters to their extraordinary articles.[48]

Tarbell and "The Oil War of 1872"

Tarbell was the first of the three to embark on her investigations, though Steffens's series began to appear in the magazine one month before Tarbell's first essay did. The decision to pursue a series of stories on the Standard Oil Company had complex beginnings. *McClure's* editor, John Finley, had approached his boss as early as 1899 with the idea of publishing several articles on the trusts. Journalist Alfred Low floated a similar, though more detailed, proposal at roughly the same time. Both men had been trained in political economy, and both had been much impressed by a conference on the trust question held by the Chicago Civic Federation in the fall of 1899. More important, both had a keen sense of the drift of public affairs. They believed that in the trust readers would find a powerful object of common concern and curiosity.[49]

That assumption was based on a firm understanding of late-nineteenth-century political economy. The 1890s had been a critical period in the great merger movement. As large businesses consolidated, they sought legal protections that would permit them to exert a controlling influence on markets and competitors. In 1882 the Standard Oil Company came up with the tactic of using the legal instrument of the trust to circumvent state antimonopoly laws that forbade one corporation from holding stock in another. Under the arrangement of the trust, stockholders of various oil companies turned over their stocks to Standard Oil "trustees." The trust in turn issued certificates to shareholders in exchange for the power to manage and direct the oil companies.

Political and legal attacks on this use of the trust forced Standard Oil to beat a hasty retreat in the early 1890s. Abandoning the trust instrument, Standard Oil instead took advantage of loosened New Jersey corporation laws to form a holding company. The holding company created a corporation whose purpose was to hold controlling stock in several other companies. The creation of Standard Oil of New Jersey, as the new holding company was known, boosted the capitalization of the corporation from $10 million to $110 million and gave it direct controlling interest in no fewer than forty-one other companies.

The attack on the trusts that was gaining steam in the 1890s was less frequently an attack on the literal legal entity of the trust. It was more often a broader effort to combat monopoly and curb the overpowering force of consolidated corporations and giant holding companies. Nonetheless the mergers continued, resulting in 1901 in the first billion-dollar corporation ever formed in the United States, U.S. Steel.[50]

It was against this backdrop that McClure began to turn over suggestions that he offer his readers a series of detailed articles on the trusts. It was true that much had already been written about this subject, but a detailed portrait studded with names and facts—the kind of portrait showcased by *McClure's*—would add something new. The question was, which trust? Standard Oil seemed an obvious choice. John D. Rockefeller's company was, in many ways, the "granddaddy" of them all and its founder a subject of no small interest as a personality. Furthermore, Tarbell's presence on the staff presented the advantage of an ace writer with intimate knowledge of the oil regions. Tarbell's father had himself fallen on some hard times since his early successes in the business. Like many independent producers, he knew what it was like to be grabbed in the stranglehold of Standard Oil, and he warned his daughter away from profiling the company in *McClure's*. "Don't do it, Ida," he cautioned. "They will ruin the magazine." At first Ida doubted that Standard Oil would care much about her essays, though she was immediately struck in beginning her research that a "persistent fog of suspicion and doubt and fear" hung over the entire subject of the great oil trust.[51]

For nearly five years Tarbell pursued her research into the history of Standard Oil. The series was originally slated as three articles, but the wealth of material uncovered and the popularity of the series justified stretching it out to nineteen essays in all, published over a period of two years. When the series ended, Tarbell's essays appeared as a book in 1904. McClure invested more than $50,000 in the project, a substantial sum of money by the standards of the day. The funds made it possible for Tarbell to hire an assistant, John Siddall, to track down leads in Cleveland, though she did much of the research herself. Indefatigable in her pursuit of missing documents, dogged in her search for personal testimony and previously untapped sources, Tarbell constructed a historical narrative whose proportions began to mirror in scale the company she detailed.

Tarbell's reliance on the public record was one of the most striking and persuasive aspects of her research. "Almost continuously since its organization in 1870," she noted, "the Standard Oil Company had been under investigation by the Congress of the United States and by the legislatures of the various states in which it had operated, on the suspicion that it was receiving rebates from the railroads and was practicing methods in restraint of free trade." Court records, the findings of state and federal investigative commissions, newspaper accounts from the oil regions, a large "pamphlet literature," and depositions from civil suits provided ample evidence of the methods Standard Oil had employed to amass its fortune and of the ways in which it maintained its monopoly.[52]

Tarbell's use of these public records was important for two reasons. First, the documents put her findings on firm evidentiary ground and thus made for persuasive reading. Tarbell uncovered some little-known Standard practices and brought together original testimony from many company intimates and industry competitors. She provided a powerful narrative structure that made a coherent whole of the company's history. But she did not so much offer entirely new intelligence on the company as collect and analyze data already in the public record. That record needed a historian with a powerful narrative voice to lift the drama of the Standard Oil story from the dreary investigating committee reports. Few Americans would bother to piece together the facts by tracking down the various fragments of evidence strewn throughout a mammoth public record. Tarbell's massive research and writing effort simplified their task, opened up what already existed, and put the public record before the public.

The painstaking character of her research and her reliance on documents was important too in protecting *McClure's Magazine* from a libel suit. As Tarbell's father warned, a libel suit in this early pass at powerful economic interests—particularly one leveled by Standard Oil—might well have "ruined" the magazine. McClure was clearly attentive to the dangers involved in Tarbell's explosive series. He hired economists John R. Commons and John Bates Clark to read portions of Tarbell's manuscript for accuracy. Every article went through repeated editorial readings, with Tarbell receiving extensive criticism from John Phillips, John Siddall, and McClure himself. These efforts and the generally high quality of Tarbell's historical research placed the magazine in a strong position had Standard Oil chosen to pursue legal redresses. The company did not do so.[53]

Another fascinating dynamic at work in Tarbell's construction of her narrative was the impact of the series itself—its announcement and then the publication of the first few articles—on the evolution of her remaining essays for *McClure's*. The series was advertised in the magazine a year after Tarbell's research had begun, and soon after S. S. McClure heard from Mark Twain that a friend of his wanted to speak to "Miss Tarbell." The friend was Henry H. Rogers, one of the most powerful Standard Oil executives. Rogers had begun his career in the industry as an independent refiner. Like so many other oil men, he had caved in to Standard Oil eventually. But he knew the oil region well and found common ground with Tarbell in their recollections of the pioneering days both remembered vividly.

For two years Rogers met regularly with Tarbell. He attempted to shape her story by giving his—and the company's—views of events. She listened politely, checked his claims against the facts, made use of what was reliable, and discarded what was not. Most important, her meetings with Rogers allowed Tarbell to penetrate the worldview of the entrepreneurs. She caught what she saw as the company's great obsession—"that nothing, however trivial, must live outside of its control." The reporter and the corporate titan "even argued with entire friendliness the debatable question, 'What is the worst thing the Standard Oil ever did?'" Rogers offered to put Tarbell in touch with other executives, including Rockefeller's founding partner and close associate Henry Flagler. Flagler proved to be a less satisfying source. Pressed by Tarbell to reveal details on Standard Oil's scheme to win rebates from the railroads, he ignored her queries and offered his own narrative history of his work with Rockefeller. As the story wound on, he punctuated his account with "we were prospered." Tarbell later dryly recalled, "That was not what I was after. Their prosperity was obvious enough." However reliable or unreliable their contents, these interviews nonetheless helped Tarbell get at the human faces behind the corporate machinations that built Standard Oil.[54]

As the series began to run in November of 1902, the public response to the articles continued to be a factor in shaping Tarbell's history. "Victims" of the company, ranging from small would-be producers to Rockefeller's estranged brother Frank, began to seek Tarbell out, regale her with horror stories, and offer additional documentary evidence. A clerk at one Standard company passed to an independent refiner damning bookkeeping records that revealed a concerted effort on the part of Standard Oil to destroy the competitor. Much impressed by the quality of Tarbell's essays he was then reading in McClure's, the refiner turned over "the full set of incriminating documents." Rogers, who had continued to cooperate through the publication of the first essays, flew into a rage when Tarbell published the damning evidence. That ended any further interviews.[55]

"The Oil War of 1872" was the third chapter of Tarbell's history to appear in *McClure's*. It tells the story of the battle independent oil producers waged against the South Improvement Company. In the 1870s, John D. Rockefeller was maneuvering to consolidate the various existing oil refiners into one huge company. One tactic used to break the competition was forged through an alliance with the railroads. In exchange for guarantees of regular, planned shipments, the refiners in the South Improvement Company would receive rebates from the railroads that reduced the cost of their shipments. In addition, they would prosper from "drawbacks"—money skimmed off the higher rates paid by those who shipped their oil without benefit of membership in the South Improvement Company. It was a devious and secretive scheme that threatened to break the backs of the independent oil producers and achieve a monopoly. There was no way producers outside the South Improvement Company could compete with a combination that could ship petroleum more cheaply than any other business in the oil region. They depended on the railroads to move crude oil out of the oil towns to outlying refineries as well as to carry crude and refined oil to distant shipping points. The South Improvement Company threatened their ability to survive in the petroleum industry.

Tarbell's father was one of the men who resisted the South Improvement Company. His daughter was a teenager during the oil war and he used the events of 1872 as a parable to teach her the importance of fair play. In spite of her personal connection to the oil war, Tarbell, in her essay for *McClure's,* presented the "facts" as she had come to understand them, believing that an objective account would best serve the evidence. She maintained the same stance throughout her *History of the Standard Oil Company.* It is worth asking how well she succeeded in this regard. Some critics accused Tarbell of harboring prejudices toward big business, independent of their corporate tactics. Does "The Oil War of 1872" support such a view? What *does* seem most troubling to Tarbell in her account of the oil war? Does she reject the realities of industrial capitalism or is she looking toward the regulation of corporations that would become one of the hallmarks of political and economic reform in the twentieth century? These are a few of the questions raised by "The Oil War of 1872."[56]

Tarbell's construction of her historical narrative also deserves scrutiny. Why might Tarbell have chosen history as her method of analyzing the great oil trust? What forces does she emphasize as causal agents? Does Tarbell see Standard Oil's monopoly as the product of the misguided genius of one man? Or does she see the struggle over oil as a contest rooted in the conditions of modern industrial society? What, in fact, is Tarbell's essential message to her readers? Why would Tarbell's account of a battle over oil that had taken place thirty years ago seem so compelling in 1903?

Steffens and "The Shame of Minneapolis"

The dripping sarcasm of Lincoln Steffens's "The Shame of Minneapolis: The Rescue and Redemption of a City That Was Sold Out" made moot any questions of strict objectivity. Political corruption was a daily news item in

Steffens's day, and the genius of his work was to bring essentially local stories of dirty politicians, corrupt police, and conspiring businessmen to a national stage. They seemed to exemplify deep flaws in the body politic and a kind of moral bankruptcy that, in Steffens's view, was infecting not just the cities but American democracy.

Steffens came to *McClure's* wise in the ways of contemporary urban politics. But *McClure's* gave him an opportunity to establish himself as one of the foremost political journalists of his day. That opportunity was, in one sense, bred of failure. Although hired to assume the duties of a managing editor, Steffens soon proved himself to be poorly suited to such administrative tasks. He also had a difficult time adjusting to his boss. S. S. McClure traveled often in search of ideas, new writers, and new material, and just as often he came home talking a blue streak to his editorial staff and raving about their failures in his absence. Steffens admired McClure tremendously, but he took "the madness of McClure's genius" to heart much more than did staff members such as Ida Tarbell who had known McClure longer and viewed him with greater sympathy.

McClure was similarly both admiring of and unhappy with his new editor. After observing Steffens in the office and looking over his editorial work, McClure sat the new arrival down and said "very sincerely, very kindly": "You may have been an editor. . . . You may be an editor. But you don't know how to edit a magazine. You must learn to." Hurt and angry, Steffens replied, "Where then can I learn? Where shall I go to learn to be an editor?" McClure "waved his hand around a wide circle," Steffens recalled. "Anywhere. Anywhere else. Get out of here, travel, go—somewhere. Go out in the advertising department. Ask them where they have transportation credit. Buy a railroad ticket, get on a train, and there, where it lands you, there you will learn to edit a magazine." The free ticket was available on a train that ran to Chicago. Steffens went there in the fall of 1902 and "learned—not exactly how to edit a magazine, but I started something which did 'make' not one but several magazines. . . . I started," Steffens boasted with less than perfect accuracy, "our political muckraking."[57]

Steffens had actually gone to Chicago with a list of contacts to query about appropriate stories for *McClure's Magazine*. One of them suggested that Steffens check out a young circuit attorney, Joseph W. Folk, whose reforming zeal was causing a stir in St. Louis politics. The crusading prosecutor was already much in the St. Louis news. Steffens saw a chance "to take confused, local, serial news of the newspapers and report it all together in one long short story for the whole country." The scene in St. Louis, Folk assured him, was "beyond belief."

In fact, as Steffens would soon stress, Folk's discovery of bribery, theft, and various other forms of corruption among the city's aldermen was well within the boundaries of belief. An unusual alliance of machine politicians and municipal reformers had put Folk in office. But once there the public prosecutor quickly learned that he was expected to heel to the demands of boss Ed Butler's Democratic machine. Rather than accede, Folk began investigating the very system that had elected him. But the "ballot stuffers" so important to the success of Butler's machine proved to be small change compared to another scandal Folk had been pursuing when Steffens met him.

In January 1902 a local reporter had called Folk's attention to an article just ten lines long in the St. Louis *Star*. The article noted that money recently deposited in a city bank was there for the purpose of paying off elected city officials in exchange for "passage of a street railroad ordinance" favorable to a railway company. Although the article mentioned no names, Folk traced the funds to the Suburban Railway Company. Within hours of publication of the article, officers of the company, bankers, lobbyists, and assemblymen were being rounded up by the sheriff at Folk's command. Claiming far more evidence than he actually had in hand, Folk frightened the railway company president and a key lobbyist into informing. An ocean of evidence then poured forth as one informer led to another and tales of routine bribes for city franchises, licenses, property, exemptions, and privileges washed over the stunned prosecutor. In spite of concerted efforts to derail him, Folk won indictments and convictions of many of the principals. The ax even "struck the greatest oak of the forest"—Colonel Ed Butler himself.[58]

When Folk met with Steffens, the former was in the midst of pursuing the trail of political and corporate corruption. Yet he willingly cooperated with the reporter because he believed national exposure could strengthen his hand in St. Louis. Initial local reaction to Folk's investigations had been disappointing; his campaign to root out corruption was written up in city newspapers "in the spirit of burlesque." As the prosecutions continued and the widespread vested interest in business as usual began to be touched, Folk believed he would lose "all local support." As a New York–based reporter, Steffens represented a safe haven for the beleaguered prosecutor. "You publish in New York," Folk stressed. "You are not subject to the pulls and the threats of St. Louis. You might see me through and so set the pace for the papers published here."[59]

Folk's canny observation underscored the mutual benefits that might accrue to political reformer and political journalist, benefits that changes in mass media made increasingly possible in the early twentieth century. Folk recognized the power of the press to mobilize public opinion. He further understood that when a national magazine made an example of St. Louis, the pressure within the city to mend its ways would be intense. National magazine exposure would elevate St. Louis politics and raise its stakes to a level that would otherwise be out of reach. Steffens's essay for *McClure's* in this sense would itself then become a weapon, however distantly wielded, in reform politics. In a stunning development that captured perfectly the shifting character of modern American society, national forces would play a powerful role in determining the local political scene.

If Folk stood to reap rewards from a profile in *McClure's Magazine,* gains for Steffens seemed ample as well. Steffens was looking for a good story, and he had one in the courage of an honorable man battling the machine. Furthermore, as he listened to Folk pour out his heart, Steffens began to see a pattern that Folk was also devastated to see. The corruption of St. Louis resembled closely the corruption Steffens had observed as a cub reporter in New York. "What Folk's mind was doing," Steffens later explained, "was simple, but unusual. He was sweeping all his cases of bribery together to form a truth out of his facts. He was generalizing." And so was Steffens. "Were not the extraordinary conditions of St. Louis and New York," he began to ask himself, "the ordinary conditions of city government in the United States?"

The two men found common ground in a second realization that was also freighted with significance. "Good business men" were in league with "bad politicians," Folk said. "It is good business that causes bad government.... It is the leading citizens that are battening on our city." This also squared well with what Steffens had seen in New York. Corrupt politics worked because it was profitable to all the players, including "the leading business men." There was more than simple or even complex crimes at work; there was a system in place that undermined the very purpose of democracy. "Bribery and corruption," Folk exclaimed, "is a process of revolution, to make a democratic government represent, not the people, but a part, the worse part of the people." "Or—the best," Steffens replied. St. Louis might be a setting for the story, Steffens decided, but the particularities of that city were just background scenery. The drama was in "the revolutionary process which was going on in all our cities." Steffens was convinced that "if I could trace it to its source, I might find the cause of political corruption—and the cure."[60]

In the meantime, more prosaic matters intervened. Steffens had found a story in St. Louis, but as an editor his duties were to match a writer to the tale. Folk recommended Charles Wetmore, a local reporter, who had been following the investigations. Steffens hired Wetmore to write the article, returned to New York, and then edited the piece when it came in. But Wetmore had soft-soaped the story in Steffens's view, and Steffens quickly began to add specifics. Fearful of his reputation, Wetmore insisted that Steffens also run his name on the piece "and take the blame" for the details he had added, if necessary. Steffens agreed and supplied a title that evoked the pattern he had come to see. "Tweed Days in St. Louis" appeared in the October 1902 issue of *McClure's Magazine.*[61]

Impressed with the St. Louis piece, McClure assigned Steffens the task of preparing a series on political corruption to run alongside Ida Tarbell's series on corporate misdeeds. Indeed, the thrust of Steffens's early work suggested considerable overlap between corruption in business and corruption in politics. A *McClure's* editor called Steffens's attention to an item on corruption in Minneapolis that had appeared in the New York *Sun*. Aware that investigations of police corruption in Minneapolis had unearthed crimes paralleling those in New York, Steffens settled on the midwestern city as the next object of research. Once again the writer picked his subject not because no one knew what was happening in the city but because "the exposure of Minneapolis was all over; the main facts had been running scrappily in the papers for a year. My job was to collect and combine the news serial into one digested, complete review." As was true in Tarbell's case, this evidentiary base grounded Steffens's exposé and provided some protection to the reputation of his magazine.

McClure provided a title for the article and an angle on the subject before Steffens had even left for Minneapolis. The essay would be called "The Shame of Minneapolis," and it would prove, McClure instructed, "that democracy is at fault; that one man has to run a city just as one man has to run a business to make it a success." Steffens firmly disagreed, but in fact he did find one man running the city, though hardly successfully. Researching the shenanigans of mayor Dr. Albert Alonzo Ames and his various police and criminal "associates," Steffens achieved a reportorial coup when he gained access to the "big mitt ledger." The ledger had been kept by gambling sharks who were set up in business by the police and others who worked for the mayor. It existed to keep track of debts owed to city officials and the police. Offered as evidence by informers, the ledger remained in the possession of the grand jury hearing evidence on the case. The foreman of the grand jury slipped the document to Steffens, who took photographs of the ledger, reproductions of which then appeared in *McClure's Magazine*. The publication of Steffens's essay on Minneapolis in January 1903 was deliberately timed by S. S. McClure to coincide with an impending mayoral election in the city. The convergence of both the reformers' and the magazine's interests in publicity once again led to an alliance that was critical to Steffens's muckraking.[62]

In reading Steffens's article, it is useful to reflect on the concerns he brought to the piece. Did Minneapolis confirm the suspicions that had taken hold during his research on St. Louis? How is his understanding of municipal political corruption altered or enlarged by what he saw in Minneapolis? Steffens hoped to find the cause of political corruption and thereby the cure. What does he offer by way of analysis and remedy in "The Shame of Minneapolis"?

It is worth thinking too about the way Steffens constructs his narrative. What tactics does he use to draw his readers in to what is, after all, a revelation of graft in a midwestern city probably never even visited by many in his audience? What makes the tale compelling and dramatic? How does the exposé compare, for shock value, with more recent investigations into corruption in contemporary politics? How might a political reporter today approach Steffens's explosive material? These are just a few of the questions raised by "The Shame of Minneapolis."

Baker and "The Right to Work"

Ray Stannard Baker's contribution to the January 1903 issue of *McClure's* added labor to complete a trio with corporate and business lawlessness. The story was inspired by a United Mine Workers strike in the anthracite coal mining fields of Pennsylvania. This strike, and Baker's response to it, must be seen within the context of the early-twentieth-century labor movement. Fiercely resisted by industry and continually crippled by a hostile judiciary, American labor unions in 1902 enjoyed little of the influence they would accrue later in the twentieth century. The United Mine Workers came the closest of any early-twentieth-century labor organization to being an exception to this rule. When measured against other labor organizations of the time, the UMW at 250,000 members was relatively powerful. In 1902 it represented 50 percent of American miners, although the union's strength was far greater in some states than in others and in the bituminous or soft coal rather than anthracite or hard coal fields. By contrast, membership in all unions in the United States had only recently passed the one-million mark: in 1900 only about 3 percent of the labor force was unionized.

At the time of the 1902 anthracite strike, the United Mine Workers had wrung important concessions, including improved hours, union recognition, and in some cases the closed shop, from bituminous mine owners. But the battle proved far more difficult in the anthracite fields. Large corporations had heavy interests in the anthracite mines, and many were determined to keep the United Mine Workers out. However strong the union was in numbers, it faced formidable opposition from anthracite mine owners who adamantly rejected recognition of the union. In May 1902 the UMW struck the anthracite mines, and a long and bloody siege ensued. There were many Slavic and Eastern European immigrants in the anthracite mines, and though much solidarity existed among the striking miners, ethnic tensions with experienced British miners complicated the strike.

Also complicating the strike was John Mitchell, leader of the United Mine Workers. Mitchell favored cooperation with business. He joined the National Civic Federation, an alliance of industrialists, labor leaders, and reformers, and secured a reputation for himself as a a "responsible" business unionist.

Mitchell had no interest in encouraging radicalism among his union member-ship, and during the anthracite strike he used his influence to dissuade bituminous miners from launching a sympathy strike. In many respects, Mitchell resembled the modern union executive as he moved among powerful financiers, government officials, and industrial capitalists. He also profited from his office as union executive. Mitchell's efforts to raise money from the miners for the purchase of his own house enraged radical labor activist Mary Harris, who was known as "Mother Jones." Relentless in her efforts to advance the coal mining rank and file, she decried union leaders' practices of "dining and wining with the aristocracy" and sitting "on velvet chairs in conference with labor's oppressors."[63]

McClure's poked its nose into the anthracite strike right from its beginnings in May 1902. Steffens prepared a sketch of Mitchell that, though not unsym-pathetic, suggested that the UMW employed strong-arm tactics not unlike those used by the trusts. By the fall, the anthracite strike was much in the news. President Roosevelt was expected to intervene, and McClure believed a good story was to be had in the coal fields. Although McClure would later give Mitchell an opportunity to explain the miners' side of the strike in the December 1902 issue of his magazine, he was eager to send a reporter to Pennsylvania to gather firsthand news.

McClure seemed particularly intrigued by the approximately 17,000 min-ers who had failed to join the UMW strike. Perhaps, as one historian has suggested, he was remembering an unsuccessful 1896 strike by pressmen against his own shop. Whatever his motivations, McClure scrambled to find a writer for the job. Tarbell was busy with her Standard Oil series, Steffens with the cities, and so it fell to Ray Stannard Baker to cover the anthracite strike. Struggling with a novel on labor, Baker agreed only reluctantly. He made his way to Wilkes Barre, Pennsylvania, in October 1902.[64]

By the time Baker arrived, Roosevelt had already appointed a commission to arbitrate the strike. Still, there was much passionate feeling among the coal miners and the many intellectuals and activists who were following the miners. Upon arrival, Baker met John Mitchell, who impressed him "not at all" as a "wild-eyed radical" but rather as a "singularly steady-headed man, with some of the qualities of both [Samuel] Gompers [president of the AFL] and [Eugene] Debs." Newspaper editor Henry Demarest Lloyd and labor lawyer Clarence Darrow were also following the strike, and Baker spent evenings in "dingy hotel bedrooms filled with tobacco smoke" listening to intense discus-sions about the miners' plight.[65]

Whether following McClure's instructions or his own lead, Baker began to visit the miners in their homes, in the fields, and in union meetings. "I used the same methods, as a reporter," he recalled, "that had proved so successful at the time of the Pullman strike in Chicago." The bitterness of the men and their vengeful attitude toward the miners who refused to walk out made a deep impression on Baker. "They hated these 'scabs,'" he observed, "to the point of murder." Though moved by the grievances of the striking miners, Baker gravitated toward the "minority" who shared the miners' harsh working conditions but refused to join their cause. The "glaring injustices of the coal fields" had already been widely publicized. There was a fresh story to be told in the perspective of the scabs.[66]

In reading Baker's account of the nonstriking miners, one must keep in mind labor's bitter and exhausting post–Civil War struggle to organize. Not until the New Deal of Franklin D. Roosevelt in the 1930s would federal legislation guarantee labor its own "bill of rights." Given that in the early twentieth century organized labor still faced considerable hostility from the courts, from industry, and from many of those who made public policy, it is worth asking why Baker chose the nonstriking miners as the focus of attention in his nationally distributed essay on the anthracite coal strike. Was Baker antilabor, as some of his critics would accuse? Or was he prescient in seeing tensions within labor that would fracture the forward movement of workers? Perhaps Baker was defending the interests of his own class—Americans of middling station who were threatened by organization of any sort. These are alternative explanations that must be sifted through.[67]

One must think too about the place of ethnicity in Baker's analysis. Does he sympathize with the nonstriking workers because they most closely resemble his own Anglo-Saxon origins? Or do his references to ethnicity simply reflect the prejudices of the nonstriking miners he interviewed? In either case, what, if anything, do Baker's comments about ethnicity reveal about the temperature in the American "melting pot" in the 1902 Pennsylvania coal fields? What, in fact, do we know from Baker's essay about any of his prejudices? McClure clearly encouraged his writers to stick to the facts. Compared with Tarbell and Steffens, does Baker succeed in presenting his findings with objectivity?

It is also important to remember in reading "The Right to Work" that it was the first of several articles Baker penned detailing labor racketeering. From Pennsylvania, he went on to Colorado and then to Chicago where he exposed what happened when "capital and labor hunt together." The Coal Teamsters Union and the Coal Team Owners Association formed an alliance in Chicago that gave labor and capital a stranglehold on the city's coal industry. Independent competition was crushed, according to Baker, and "the defenseless, unorganized public paid the bill." By the fall of 1903, Baker was back in New York covering the building trade strike. There the leader of 4,500 unionized building workers defied all notions that organized labor was represented by advocates of the rank and file. Instead the union leader "was riding about in his cab, wearing diamonds, appearing on the street with his blooded bulldog, supporting his fast horses, 'treating' his friends." Funds siphoned from the "union treasury" didn't begin to match the bribes that Sam Parks, the corrupt union boss, was being paid by "builders and manufacturers." Indeed, Baker's digging revealed that while employed by the union to represent their interest, Parks was also employed by the Fuller Company, a large corporation "backed by representatives of the Standard Oil Company, the United States Steel Corporation, and many of the greatest railroad corporations."[68]

Baker began to conclude that the resistance of some corporations to organized labor masked an insidious new trend in labor management. A company might recognize "the rights of labor," only to continue to exploit workers *as a union*. As Baker continued his investigations, and as he came to the conclusions being reached by Steffens and Tarbell, he began to see a pattern in all of their stories. "Where bribes were received bribes must be paid." The trail of labor racketeering led back to business. The corruption in the labor unions represented merely another manifestation of "an invisible germ . . . which was circulating in the blood of the American people." Labor racketeering was not a lamentable anomaly in an otherwise robust society. It represented, Baker concluded with deep distress, *"the American way of life in many of its most important activities."*[69]

S. S. McClure's editorial that accompanied the three muckraking articles, the last of the documents gathered here, spells out that sentiment for the readers of his magazine. The excitement in the editorial offices of *McClure's* must have been intense as Tarbell, Steffens, and Baker began to submit their essays. The genius of McClure had played an important part in the evolution of each of his writer's articles. In that sense, he could not have been surprised that when put together the essays formed a most impressive whole. Yet McClure deliberately selected the three essays reprinted here for the January 1903 issue of the magazine even though he could not have predicted that Tarbell's, Steffens's, and Baker's findings would make such a powerful collective statement about American society.

McClure's decision to run an editorial calling attention to the three essays was unusual—and unusually effective. The editor dragged out his sledge hammer to make sure the reader knew that what he called a "coincidence" in magazine editing was no coincidence in American society and politics. As short as McClure's editorial was, it provided a framework for the three essays as well as a call to arms to the American public. Corruption and lawlessness were pandemic, and to every American belonged responsibility. Was this a fitting summary of the views of Tarbell, Steffens, and Baker? Or do McClure's comments suggest that the editor had a different perspective on his reporters' tales of American society? A final question to consider: Had McClure *not* run the editorial, would the January 1903 issue of *McClure's* have been given credit for launching muckraking in the magazines? That is "a coincidence that may set us thinking" as well.[70]

NOTES

[1]Frank L. Mott, *A History of American Magazines* (Cambridge: Harvard University Press, 1957), 4:599; Louis Filler, *The Muckrakers* (University Park, Pa.: Pennsylvania State University Press, 1976), 82–83; Harold S. Wilson, *McClure's Magazine and the Muckrakers* (Princeton: Princeton University Press, 1970), 146–47.

[2]Arthur and Lila Weinberg, *The Muckrakers* (New York: Simon and Schuster, 1961), 58–59; John E. Semonche, "Theodore Roosevelt's 'Muck-Rake Speech': A Reassessment," *Mid-America* 46, no. 2 (April 1964): 114–25.

[3]Filler, *Muckrakers,* chaps. 5 and 6; Josiah Flynt, "In the World of Graft," *McClure's Magazine* 16 (February 1901): 327–34; C. C. Regier, *The Era of the Muckrakers* (Chapel Hill: University of North Carolina Press, 1932), chaps. 3–5; Claude H. Wetmore and Lincoln Steffens, "Tweed Days in New York," *McClure's Magazine* 22 (October 1902); Ida M. Tarbell, "History of the Standard Oil Company," *McClure's Magazine* 22 (November and December 1902).

[4]Justin Kaplan, *Lincoln Steffens: A Biography* (New York: Simon and Schuster, 1974), 112–15; David M. Chalmers, *The Social and Political Ideas of the Muckrakers* (New York: Citadel Press, 1964), 15.

[5]For good overviews of developments in late-nineteenth-century politics and society, see Samuel P. Hays, *The Response to Industrialism, 1885–1914* (Chicago: University of Chicago Press, 1957); Robert H. Wiebe, *The Search for Order, 1877–1920* (New York: Hill and Wang, 1967); Nell Irvin Painter, *Standing at Armageddon: The United States, 1877–1919* (New York: Norton, 1987); and Morton Keller, *Affairs of State: Public Life in Late Nineteenth Century America* (Cambridge: Harvard University Press, 1977).

[6]Hays, *Response to Industrialism,* chap. 3; Alfred D. Chandler, *The Visible Hand: The Managerial Revolution in American Business* (Cambridge: Harvard University Press, 1977), chaps. 3, 10; Glen Porter, *The Rise of Big Business, 1860–1910* (New York: Thomas Y. Crowell Company, 1973), 31–39, 71–84; Keller, *Affairs of State,* chaps. 5, 10, 11; Morton Keller, *Regulating a New Economy: Public Policy and Economic Change in America, 1900–1933* (Cambridge: Harvard University Press, 1990), 24 and *passim;* Naomi Lamoureaux, *The Great Merger Movement in American Business, 1895–1904* (Cambridge: Harvard University Press, 1985); Wiebe, *Search for Order,* chap. 2. The laissez-faire economy was the relatively unregulated state of American capitalism in the late nineteenth century. The doctrine of laissez-faire posited the existence of natural laws regulating the economy. If unfettered by government and by constraints on investment and trade, the natural workings of the economy would ensure the advancement of wealth and the common good, according to classical economics.

[7]Quote from Ida M. Tarbell, *All in the Day's Work* (New York: Macmillan, 1939), 82; David Brody, *Steelworkers in America: The Nonunion Era* (New York: Harper, 1960), 37–40; Price V. Fishback, *Soft Coal, Hard Choices: The Economic Welfare of Bituminous Coal Miners, 1890–1930* (New York: Oxford University Press, 1992), 102–8; Chandler, *Visible Hand,* 170–75, 325–29; Porter, *Rise of Big Business,* 80–85 and *passim.*

[8]David Montgomery, *The Fall of the House of Labor: The Workplace, the State, and American Labor Activism, 1865–1925* (Cambridge: Cambridge University Press, 1987); Herbert G. Gutman, *Work, Culture, and Society in Industrializing America* (New York: Vintage, 1977); Melvyn Dubofsky, *Industrialism and the American Worker, 1865–1920* (Arlington Heights, Ill.: AHM

Publishing, 1975); Alexander Keyssar, *Out of Work: The First Century of Unemployment in Massachusetts* (Cambridge: Cambridge University Press, 1986).

[9]Keller, *Affairs of State;* Theda Skocpol, *Protecting Soldiers and Mothers: The Political Origins of Social Policy in the United States* (Cambridge: Harvard University Press, 1992); Richard L. McCormick, "The Discovery That Business Corrupts Politics: A Reappraisal of the Origins of Progressivism," *American Historical Review* 86 (1981): 247–74; Michael E. McGerr, *The Decline of Popular Politics* (New York: Oxford University Press, 1986); John C. Teaford, *The Unheralded Triumph: City Government in America, 1870–1900* (Baltimore: Johns Hopkins University Press, 1984); John Garrity, *The American Nation* (New York: Harper and Row, 1979), 513.

[10]Tarbell, *All in the Day's Work,* 82; Hays, *Response to Industrialism;* Sidney Fine, *Laissez-Faire and the General Welfare State* (Ann Arbor: University of Michigan Press, 1967).

[11]Filler, *Muckrakers,* chap. 2; Keller, *Affairs of State,* chap. 8; Ronald Yanosky, "Seeing the Cat: Henry George and the Rise of the Single Tax Movement, 1879–1890," Ph.D. dissertation, University of California at Berkeley, 1993; John L. Thomas, *Alternative America: Henry George, Edward Bellamy, Henry Demarest Lloyd, and the Adversary Tradition* (Cambridge: Harvard University Press, 1983). The mugwumps were independent Republicans who bolted from their party in 1884 to support Democratic reform governor of New York Grover Cleveland for the presidency. They criticized the party system and agitated for good government and "morality in politics." Newspaperwriters were highly visible in the movement. Keller, *Affairs of State,* 550–52.

[12]Dorothy Ross, *The Origins of American Social Science* (Cambridge: Cambridge University Press, 1991); James T. Kloppenberg, *Uncertain Victory: Social Democracy and Progressivism in European and American Thought, 1870–1920* (New York: Oxford University Press, 1986); Martin Bulmer, Kevin Bales, and Kathryn Kish Sklar, *The Social Survey in Historical Perspective, 1880–1940* (Cambridge: Cambridge University Press, 1991); Ellen Fitzpatrick, *Endless Crusade: Women Social Scientists and Progressive Reform* (New York: Oxford University Press, 1990).

[13]Mott, *History of American Magazines* 4:1–11; Keller, *Affairs of State,* 290–93; Filler, *Muckrakers,* 16; Christopher P. Wilson, *The Labor of Words: Literary Professionalism in the Progressive Era* (Athens: University of Georgia Press, 1985), 43–46.

[14]Filler, *Muckrakers,* 16; McGerr, *Decline of Popular Politics,* 107–36; Mott, *History of American Magazines,* vol. 4, chap. 1; Wilson, *McClure's Magazine,* chap. 2; Keller, *Affairs of State,* 566; Frank L. Mott, "The Magazine Revolution and Popular Ideas in the Nineties," *American Antiquarian Society Proceedings* 64 (1954): 195–214; Beaumont Newhall, *The History of Photography* (New York: Museum of Modern Art, 1964), 175–78.

[15]Mott, *History of American Magazines* 4:2–5, 589–90; Filler, *Muckrakers,* 34–42; Wilson, *McClure's Magazine,* 62–65; Richard S. Tedlow, *New and Improved: The Story of Mass Marketing in America* (New York: Basic Books, 1990), chap. 1; John Tebbel and Mary Ellen Zuckerman, *The Magazine in America, 1741–1990* (New York: Oxford University Press, 1991), 66.

[16]Wiebe, *Search for Order,* chaps. 3, 5, 6; Lawrence Levine, *Highbrow/Lowbrow* (Cambridge: Harvard University Press, 1988).

[17]Newhall, *History of Photography,* 135–42, 175–80.

[18]Wilson, *McClure's Magazine,* chaps. 4, 5; Mott, *History of American Magazines* 4:589–607; Wilson, *Labor of Words,* 57.

[19]Mott, *History of American Magazines* 4:590–93, 598–99; Tarbell, *All in the Day's Work,* chap. 1; Wilson, *McClure's Magazine,* 66–69; Filler, *Muckrakers,* 36–37.

[20]Tarbell, *All in the Day's Work,* 11–12.

[21]Ibid., 5–6, 9; Daniel Yergin, *The Prize: The Epic Quest for Oil, Money, and Power* (New York: Simon and Schuster, 1992), 101–2.

[22]Tarbell, *All in the Day's Work,* 4–9, 12–14.

[23]Ibid., 34–36, 40–64; Wilson, *McClure's Magazine,* 68; Kathleen Brady, *Ida M. Tarbell: Portrait of a Muckraker* (New York: Sea View/Putnam, 1984), chap. 2.

[24]Tarbell, *All in the Day's Work,* chap. 5; Wilson, *McClure's Magazine,* 68–69.

[25]Tarbell, *All in the Day's Work,* 84–114; Brady, *Ida M. Tarbell,* 44–45, 60–61.

[26]Tarbell, *All in the Day's Work,* 120–46.

[27]Ibid., 96–99, 118–24, chap. 8; Wilson, *McClure's Magazine,* 69–73; Mott, *History of American Magazines* 4:589–91.

[28]Wilson, *McClure's Magazine*, 64–65, 73–75; Mott, *History of American Magazines* 4:590–91, 596, 599. There is some small discrepancy between Mott and Wilson on these circulation figures. In this instance I have relied most on Wilson, who cites archival sources.

[29]Tarbell, *All in the Day's Work*, 189–97; Wilson, *McClure's Magazine*, 88–89; Mott, *History of American Magazines* 4:596.

[30]Robert C. Bannister, *Ray Stannard Baker: The Mind and Thought of a Progressive* (New Haven: Yale University Press, 1966), 1–20, 24–40; Wilson, *McClure's Magazine*, 85.

[31]Ray Stannard Baker, *American Chronicle: The Autobiography of Ray Stannard Baker* (New York: Charles Scribner's Sons, 1945), 1–2; Ray Ginger, *Altgeld's America: Chicago from 1892–1905* (New York: Markus Wiener Publishing, 1986).

[32]Baker, *American Chronicle*, 6–25, 34–41; Wilson, *McClure's Magazine*, 85–86; Bannister, *Ray Stannard Baker*, 46–54.

[33]Baker, *American Chronicle*, 11–12, 18–19, 42–43, and *passim;* Wilson, *McClure's Magazine*, 107–8; Mott, *History of American Magazines* 4:590–93.

[34]Baker, *American Chronicle*, 31, 45; Bannister, *Ray Stannard Baker*, 41–54.

[35]Baker, *American Chronicle*, 73, 81; Tarbell, *All in the Day's Work*, 196–97; Wilson, *McClure's Magazine*, 87–88.

[36]Baker, *American Chronicle*, 84–85, 87–90, 115–18, 120–22, chap. 12; Wilson, *McClure's Magazine*, 115–16, 88–89; Bannister, *Ray Stannard Baker*, 78–79; Ray Stannard Baker, "What the U.S. Steel Corporation Really Is," *McClure's Magazine* 18 (November 1901); Ray Stannard Baker, "The Great Northern Pacific Deal," *Collier's Weekly* 28 (30 Nov. 1901). The latter essay was first written for *McClure's*, which rejected the piece.

[37]Tarbell, *All in the Day's Work*, 198–99; Lincoln Steffens, *The Autobiography of Lincoln Steffens* (New York: Harcourt Brace, 1931), 1:4, 102–11, chaps. 2, 4; Kaplan, *Lincoln Steffens*, chap. 1; Wilson, *McClure's Magazine*, 89–90.

[38]Steffens, *Autobiography*, 124, 118, 132, chaps. 16–18 *passim*.

[39]Steffens, *Autobiography*, 149, 152, chaps. 18–21 *passim;* Kaplan, *Lincoln Steffens*, 45–46; Wilson, *McClure's Magazine*, 90; Jurgen Herbst, *The German Historical School in American Scholarship* (Ithaca: Cornell University Press, 1965).

[40]Steffens, *Autobiography*, 169, chaps. 22, 23 *passim;* Wilson, *McClure's Magazine*, 90.

[41]Steffens, *Autobiography*, 187; Wilson, *McClure's Magazine*, 91–92; Kaplan, *Lincoln Steffens*, 53–57.

[42]Steffens, *Autobiography*, pp. 236–37, 256–57.

[43]Ibid., chaps. 4–14 *passim;* Terrence J. McDonald, ed., *Plunkitt of Tammany Hall* (Boston: Bedford Books, 1993); Wilson, *McClure's Magazine*, 91–92; Keller, *Affairs of State*, 290–91.

[44]Steffens, *Autobiography*, 203–7, 223, 315, chap. 10 *passim;* Wilson, *McClure's Magazine*, 92–93.

[45]Steffens, *Autobiography*, 344, chap. 11 *passim*.

[46]Ibid., 358–59.

[47]Kaplan, *Lincoln Steffens*, 117; Bannister, *Ray Stannard Baker*, chaps. 3, 4 *passim*.

[48]"Concerning Three Articles in This Number of McClure's, and a Coincidence That May Set Us Thinking," *McClure's Magazine* 20, no. 3 (January 1903): 336.

[49]Wilson, *McClure's Magazine*, 132–37; McCormick, "Discovery," 259; Tarbell, *All in the Day's Work*, 202–7.

[50]Keller, *Affairs of State*, 435–38; Yergin, *The Prize*, 44–47, 97–98; Hays, *Response to Industrialism*, 50; Chandler, *Visible Hand, passim*.

[51]Tarbell, *All in the Day's Work*, 206–7; Wilson, *McClure's Magazine*, 129–42.

[52]Mott, *History of American Magazines* 4:598; Tarbell, *All in the Day's Work*, 207, chap. 11 *passim;* Brady, *Ida M. Tarbell*, 125–38.

[53]Chalmers, *Social and Political Ideas*, 14 and *passim;* Brady, *Ida M. Tarbell*, 132–35.

[54]Tarbell, *All in the Day's Work*, 211–19.

[55]Ibid., 226–28, 237–38.

[56]Yergin, *The Prize*, 39–43; Tarbell, *All in the Day's Work*, 23–25, 218–20; Ida M. Tarbell, "The Oil War of 1872," *McClure's Magazine* 20, no. 3 (January 1903): 248–60.

[57]Steffens, *Autobiography*, 363–64; Wilson, *McClure's Magazine*, 140–44.

[58]Steffens, *Autobiography,* 368–71, vol. 2, chap. 2 *passim;* Lincoln Steffens, *The Shame of the Cities* (New York: Hill and Wang, 1985), 39.

[59]Steffens, *Shame of the Cities,* 28; Steffens, *Autobiography,* 369.

[60]Steffens, *Autobiography,* 371–73.

[61]Ibid., 372–73.

[62]Ibid., 374–78; Wilson, *McClure's Magazine,* 143–44.

[63]Fishback, *Soft Coal, Hard Choices,* 23–25, 89–90; James R. Green, *The World of the Worker* (New York: Hill and Wang, 1980), 51–56; Arthur E. Suffern, *The Coal Miners' Struggle for Industrial Status* (New York: Macmillan, 1926), 85–94; Montgomery, *Fall of the House of Labor,* 264; Elizabeth Levy and Tad Richards, *Struggle and Lose, Struggle and Win: The United Mine Workers* (New York: Four Winds Press, 1977).

[64]Wilson, *McClure's Magazine,* 144–45, 144 n. 71; Bannister, *Ray Stannard Baker,* 86–87.

[65]Baker, *American Chronicle,* 166–67. Though Clarence Darrow was known for his work as a labor lawyer in 1903, he later achieved much fame for his extraordinary skill as a criminal defense attorney.

[66]Baker, *American Chronicle,* 167.

[67]Green, *World of the Worker;* Montgomery, *Fall of the House of Labor;* Dubofsky, *Industrialism and the American Worker;* William E. Forbath, *Law and the Shaping of the American Labor Movement* (Cambridge: Harvard University Press, 1991).

[68]Baker, *American Chronicle,* 173–82.

[69]Ibid., 176–78.

[70]Wilson, *McClure's Magazine,* 146–52.

The Documents

Fall and Redemption of Minneapolis

McCLURE'S
MAGAZINE

FOR JANUARY 1903

PUBLISHED MONTHLY BY THE S.S. McCLURE CO., 141-155 E. 25th ST., NEW YORK CITY
10 Norfolk St., Strand, London, W.C., Eng. Copyright, 1902, by The S. S. McClure Co. Entered at N.Y. Post Office as Second Class Matter

McClure's Magazine

VOL. XX   *JANUARY, 1903*   NO. 3

THE SHAME OF MINNEAPOLIS

The Rescue and Redemption of a City that was Sold Out

BY LINCOLN STEFFENS

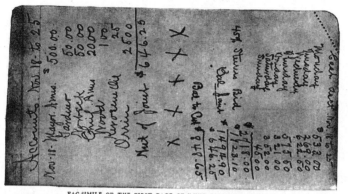

FAC-SIMILE OF THE FIRST PAGE OF "THE BIG MITT LEDGER"

An account kept by a swindler of the dealings of his "Joint" with City Officials, showing first payments made to Mayor Ames, his brother, the Chief of Police and Detectives. This book figured in trials and newspaper reports of the exposure, but was "lost"; and its whereabouts was the mystery of the proceedings. This is the first glimpse that any one, except "Cheerful Charlie" Howard, who kept it, and members of the grand jury, has had of the book

The *"Shame of Minneapolis"* was the second of Lincoln Steffens's six articles on urban political corruption for McClure's. In this essay he offers a gripping tale of a city run over with deceitful politicians, crooked police, crafty swindlers, and petty thieves. At the center of the drama are Doc Ames, the venal four-term mayor of Minneapolis, and the courageous grand jury foreman Hovey Clarke, who dared to take on the mayor's gang. (See pages 31–32 of the Introduction for some questions raised by Steffens's essay.)

Left: The cover of the January 1903 issue of *McClure's Magazine.*
Above: The masthead and opening page of the January 1903 issue of *McClure's Magazine.*

Whenever anything extraordinary is done in American municipal politics, whether for good or for evil, you can trace it almost invariably to one man. The people do not do it. Neither do the "gangs," "combines," or political parties. These are but instruments by which bosses (not leaders: we Americans are not led, but driven) rule the people, and commonly sell them out. But there are at least two forms of the autocracy which has supplanted the democracy here as it has everywhere it has been tried. One is that of the organized majority by which, as in Tammany Hall[1] in New York and the Republican machine in Philadelphia, the boss has normal control of more than half the voters. The other is that of the adroitly managed minority. The "good people" are herded into parties and stupefied with convictions and a name, Republican or Democrat; while the "bad people" are so organized or interested by the boss that he can wield their votes to enforce terms with party managers and decide elections. St. Louis is a conspicuous example of this form. Minneapolis is another. Colonel Ed. Butler is the unscrupulous opportunist who handled the non-partisan minority which turned St. Louis into a "boodle town."[2] In Minneapolis "Doc" Ames was the man.

Minneapolis is a New England town on the upper Mississippi. The metropolis of the Northwest, it is the metropolis also of Norway and Sweden in America. Indeed, it is the second largest Scandinavian city in the world. But Yankees, straight from Down East, settled the town, and their New England spirit predominates. They had Bayard Taylor[3] lecture there in the early days of the settlement; they made it the seat of the University of Minnesota. Yet even now, when the town has grown to a population of more than 200,000, you feel that there is something Western about it too—a Yankee with a small Puritan head, an open prairie heart, and a great, big Scandinavian body. The Roundhead[4] takes the Swede and Norwegian bone out into the woods, and they cut lumber by forests, or they go out on the prairies and raise wheat and mill it into fleet-cargoes of flour. They work hard, they make money, they are sober, satisfied, busy with their own affairs. There isn't much time for public business. Taken together, Miles, Hans, and Ole are very American. Miles insists upon strict laws, Ole and Hans want one or two Scandinavians on their ticket. These things granted, they go off on raft or reaper, leaving whose will to enforce the laws and run the city.

[1]Tammany Hall refers to the faction of New York City's Democratic party that had built up a powerful political machine, controlled by the Irish, by the late nineteenth century. Tammany Hall was also a building owned by a benevolent group called the Tammany Society. The political machine rented space in Tammany Hall and there was important overlap in membership between the benevolent society and the political faction.

[2]"Boodle" was bribe money. Steffens means here that St. Louis has been turned into a town rife with political corruption.

[3]A popular nineteenth-century American poet.

[4]Puritan.

Hovey C. Clarke
Foreman of the grand jury which cleaned out Mayor Ames's administration, caught and had convicted the officials who sold criminal rights to loot Minneapolis

The people who were left to govern the city hated above all things strict laws. They were the loafers, saloon keepers, gamblers, criminals, and the thriftless poor of all nationalities. Resenting the sobriety of a staid, industrious community, and having no Irish to boss them, they delighted to follow the jovial pioneer doctor, Albert Alonzo Ames. He was the "good fellow"—a genial, generous reprobate. Devery,[5] Tweed,[6] and many more have exposed in vain this amiable type. "Doc" Ames, tall, straight, and cheerful, attracted men,

[5] William S. Devery was a corrupt New York City chief of police who did the bidding of Richard Croker, boss of Tammany Hall. Steffens wrote articles exposing Devery when the reporter was working for the *Commercial Advertiser*.
[6] William Marcy Tweed, infamous political boss of Tammany Hall.

and they gave him votes for his smiles. He stood for license. There was nothing of the Puritan about him. His father, the sturdy old pioneer, Dr. Alfred Elisha Ames, had a strong strain of it in him, but he moved on with his family of six sons from Garden Prairie, Ill., to Fort Snelling reservation, in 1851, before Minneapolis was founded, and young Albert Alonzo, who then was ten years old, grew up free, easy, and tolerant. He was sent to school, then to college in Chicago, and he returned home a doctor of medicine before he was twenty-one. As the town waxed soberer and richer, "Doc" grew gayer and more and more generous. Skilful as a surgeon, devoted as a physician, and as a man kindly, he increased his practice till he was the best-loved man in the community. He was especially good to the poor. Anybody could summon "Doc" Ames at any hour to any distance. He went, and he gave not only his professional service, but sympathy, and often charity. "Richer men than you will pay your bill," he told the destitute. So there was a basis for his "goodfellowship." There always is; these good fellows are not frauds—not in the beginning.

But there is another side to them sometimes. Ames was sunshine not to the sick and destitute only. To the vicious and the depraved also he was a comfort. If a man was a hard drinker, the good Doctor cheered him with another drink; if he had stolen something, the Doctor helped to get him off. He was naturally vain; popularity developed his love of approbation. His loose life brought disapproval only from the good people, so gradually the Doctor came to enjoy best the society of the barroom and the streets. This society, flattered in turn, worshipped the good Doctor, and, active in politics always, put its physician into the arena.

Had he been wise, or even shrewd, he might have made himself a real power. But he wasn't calculating, only light and frivolous, so he did not organize his forces and run men for office. He sought office himself from the start, and he got most of the small places he wanted by changing his party to seize the opportunity. His floating minority, added to the regular partisan vote, was sufficient ordinarily for his useless victories. As time went on he rose from smaller offices to be a Republican mayor, then twice at intervals to be a Democratic mayor. He was a candidate once for Congress; he stood for governor once on a sort of Populist-Democrat ticket. Ames could not get anything outside of his own town, and after his third term as mayor it was thought he was out of politics altogether. He was getting old, and he was getting worse.

Like many a "good fellow" with hosts of miscellaneous friends down town to whom he was devoted, the good Doctor neglected his own family. From neglect he went on openly to separation from his wife and a second establishment. The climax came not long before the election of 1900. His wife was dying, and his daughter wrote to her father a note saying that her mother

Mayor A. A. Ames

The "moral leper," who, known to everybody in Minneapolis for what he was, was four times elected mayor; head of a system of robbery, blackmail, and plunder conducted by professional criminals under police direction

wished to see and forgive him. The messenger found him in a saloon. The Doctor read the note, laid it on the bar, and scribbled across it a sentence incredibly obscene. His wife died. The outraged family would not have the father at the funeral, but he appeared, not at the house, but in a carriage on the street. He sat across the way, with his feet up and a cigar in his mouth, till the funeral moved; then he circled around, crossing it and meeting it, and making altogether a scene which might well close any man's career.

It didn't end his. The people had just secured the passage of a new primary law to establish direct popular government. There were to be no more nominations by convention. The voters were to ballot for their party candidates. By a slip of some sort, the laws did not specify that Republicans only should vote for Republican candidates, and only Democrats for Democratic candidates. Any voter could vote at either primary. Ames, in disrepute with his own party, the Democratic, bade his followers vote for his nomination for mayor on the Republican ticket. They all voted; not all the Republicans did. He was nominated. Nomination is far from election, and you would say that the trick would not help him. But that was a Presidential year, so the people of Minneapolis had to vote for Ames, the Republican candidate for Mayor. Besides, Ames said he was going to reform; that he was getting old, and wanted to close his career with a good administration. The effective argument, however, was that, since McKinley had to be elected to save the country, Ames must be supported for Mayor of Minneapolis. Why? The great American people cannot be trusted to scratch a ticket.[7]

Well, Minneapolis got its old mayor back, and he was reformed. Up to this time Ames had not been very venal personally. He was a "spender," not a "grafter," and he was guilty of corruption chiefly by proxy; he took the honors and left the spoils to his followers. His administrations were no worse than the worst. Now, however, he set out upon a career of corruption which for deliberateness, invention, and avarice has never been equalled. It was as if he had made up his mind that he had been careless long enough, and meant to enrich his last years. He began early.

Immediately upon his election, before he took office (on January 7th), he organized a cabinet and laid plans to turn the city over to outlaws who were to work under police direction for the profit of his administration. He chose for chief his brother, Colonel Fred W. Ames, who had recently returned under a cloud from service in the Philippines. The Colonel had commanded a Minnesota regiment out there till he proved a coward under fire; he escaped court-martial only on the understanding that he should resign on reaching San Francisco, whither he was immediately shipped. This he did not do, and his brother's influence at Washington saved him to be mustered out with the regiment. But he was a weak vessel for chief of police, and the mayor picked for chief of detectives an abler man, who was to direct the more difficult

---

[7]"To scratch a ticket" refers in today's parlance to split-ticket voting—selecting candidates from more than one political party. Steffens here expresses his discouragement over the tendency of citizens to vote along strict party lines. At the turn of the century many states continued the common nineteenth-century practice of grouping the names of candidates by political party rather than listing the office first and then the names of electoral candidates. Before the Civil War it was necessary to scratch out the name of a candidate on the party slate a voter did not want to endorse. The phrase "to scratch a ticket" came to mean to split one's votes.

operations. This was Norman W. King, a former gambler, who knew the criminals needed in the business ahead. King was to invite to Minneapolis thieves, confidence men, pickpockets, and gamblers, and release some that were in the local jail. They were to be organized into groups, according to their profession, and detectives were assigned to assist and direct them. The head of the gambling syndicate was to have charge of the gambling, making the terms and collecting the "graft," just as King and a Captain Hill were to collect from the thieves. The collector for women of the town was to be Irwin A. Gardner, a medical student in the Doctor's office, who was made a special policeman for the purpose. These men looked over the force, selected those men who could be trusted, charged them a price for their retention, and marked for dismissal 107 men out of 225, the 107 being the best policemen in the department from the point of view of the citizens who afterward reorganized the force. John Fitchette, better known as "Coffee John," a Virginian (who served on the Jeff Davis[8] jury), the keeper of a notorious coffee-house, was to be a captain of police with no duties except to sell places on the police force.

And they did these things that they planned—all and more. The administration opened with the revolution on the police force. They liberated the thieves in the local jail, and made known to the Under World generally that "things were doing" in Minneapolis. The incoming swindlers reported to King or his staff for instructions, and went to work, turning the "swag"[9] over to the detectives in charge. Gambling went on openly, and disorderly houses multiplied under the fostering care of Gardner, the medical student. But all this was not enough. Ames dared to break openly into the municipal system of vice protection.

There was such a thing. Minneapolis, strict in its laws, forbade vices which are inevitably, then regularly permitted them under certain conditions. Legal limits, called "patrol lines," were prescribed, within which saloons might be opened. These ran along the river front, out through part of the business section, with long arms reaching into the Scandinavian quarters, north and south. Gambling also was confined, but more narrowly. And there were limits, also arbitrary, but not always identical with those for gambling, within which the social evil[10] was allowed. But the novel feature of this scheme was that disorderly houses were practically licensed by the city, the women appearing before the clerk of the Municipal Court each month to pay a "fine" of $100. Unable at first to get this "graft," Ames's man Gardner persuaded women to start houses, apartments, and, of all things, candy stores, which sold sweets

---

[8]Jefferson Davis was president of the Confederacy. Steffens refers here to the grand jury that indicted Davis for treason in 1866. Though Davis was imprisoned, the case never went to trial.
[9]"Swag" in this context means loot.
[10]Prostitution.

to children and tobacco to the "lumber Jacks" in front, while a nefarious traffic was carried on in the rear. But they paid Ames, not the city, and that was all the reform administration cared about.

The revenue from all these sources must have been enormous. It only whetted the avarice of the mayor and his Cabinet. They let gambling privileges without restriction to location or "squareness"; the syndicate could cheat and rob as it would. Peddlers and pawnbrokers, formerly licensed by the city, bought permits now instead from "Gardner's father," A. L. Gardner, who was the mayor's agent in this field. Some two hundred slot machines were installed in various parts of the town, with owner's agent and mayor's agent watching and collecting from them enough to pay the mayor $15,000 a year as his share. Auction frauds were instituted. Opium joints and unlicensed saloons, called "blind pigs," were protected. Gardner even had a police baseball team, for whose games tickets were sold to people who had to buy them. But the women were the easiest "graft." They were compelled to buy illustrated biographies of the city officials; they had to give presents of money, jewelry, and gold stars to police officers. But the money they still paid direct to the city in fines, some $35,000 a year, fretted the mayor, and at last he reached for it. He came out with a declaration, in his old character as friend of the oppressed, that $100 a month was too much for these women to pay. They should be required to pay the city fine only once in two months. This puzzled the town till it became generally known that Gardner collected the other month for the mayor. The final outrage in this department, however, was an order of the mayor for the periodic visits to disorderly houses, by the city's physicians, at from $5 to $20 per visit. The two physicians he appointed called when they willed, and more and more frequently, till toward the end the calls became a pure formality, with the collections as the one and only object.

In a general way all this business was known. It did not arouse the citizens, but it did attract criminals, and more and more thieves and swindlers came hurrying to Minneapolis. Some of them saw the police, and made terms. Some were seen by the police and invited to go to work. There was room for all. This astonishing fact that the government of a city asked criminals to rob the people is fully established. The police and the criminals have confessed it separately. Their statements agree in detail. Detective Norbeck made the arrangement, and introduced the swindlers to Gardner, who, over King's head, took the money from them. Here is the story "Billy" Edwards, a "big mitt"[11] man, told under oath of his reception in Minneapolis:

---

[11]The "big mitt" referred to a card game of stud poker in which players were swindled by one who held a stacked hand. In this context, Steffens is referring to a ring of swindlers, gamblers, and thieves who were being protected and assisted by corrupt police and politicians in Minneapolis. The "big mitt" ledger was the record compiled by the participants showing earnings and payments. When Steffens gained access to the "big mitt" ledger, it clinched his investigative work.

"I had been out to the coast, and hadn't seen Norbeck for some time. After I returned I boarded a Minneapolis car one evening to go down to South Minneapolis to visit a friend. Norbeck and Detective DeLaittre were on the car. When Norbeck saw me he came up and shook hands, and said, 'Hullo, Billy, how goes it?' I said, 'Not very well.' Then he says, 'Things have changed since you went away. Me and Gardner are the whole thing now. Before you left they thought I didn't know anything, but I turned a few tricks, and now I'm It.' 'I'm glad of that, Chris,' I said. He says, 'I've got great things for you. I'm going to fix up a joint for you.' 'That's good,' I said, 'but I don't believe you can do it.' 'Oh, yes, I can,' he replied. 'I'm It now—Gardner and me.' 'Well, if you can do it,' says I, 'there's money in it.' 'How much can you pay?' he asked. 'Oh, $150 or $200 a week,' says I. 'That settles it,' he said; 'I'll take you down to see Gardner, and we'll fix it up.' Then he made an appointment to meet me the next night, and we went down to Gardner's house together."

There Gardner talked business in general, showed his drawer full of bills, and jokingly asked how Edwards would like to have them. Edwards says:

"I said, 'That looks pretty good to me,' and Gardner told us that he had 'collected' the money from the women he had on his staff, and that he was going to pay it over to the 'old man' when he got back from his hunting trip next morning. Afterward he told me that the mayor had been much pleased with our $500, and that he said everything was all right, and for us to go ahead."

"Link" Crossman, another confidence man who was with Edwards, said that Gardner demanded $1,000 at first, but compromised on $500 for the mayor, $50 for Gardner, and $50 for Norbeck. To the chief, Fred Ames, they gave tips now and then of $25 or $50. "The first week we ran," said Crossman, "I gave Fred $15. Norbeck took me down there. We shook hands, and I handed him an envelope with $15. He pulled out a list of steerers[12] we had sent him, and said he wanted to go over them with me. He asked where the joint was located. At another time I slipped $25 into his hand as he was standing in the hallway of City Hall." But these smaller payments, after the first "opening, $500," are all down on the pages of the "big mitt" ledger, photographs of which illuminate this article. This notorious book, which was kept by Charlie Howard, one of the "big mitt" men, was much talked of at the subsequent trials, but was kept hidden to await the trial of the mayor himself.

The "big mitt" game was swindling by means of a stacked hand at stud poker. "Steerers" and "boosters" met "suckers" on the street, at hotels, and railway stations, won their confidence, and led them to the "joint." Usually the "sucker" was called, by the amount of his loss, "the $102 man" or "the $35

---

[12]"Steerers" were men hired by the ring who literally "steered" unsuspecting victims off the streets to the secret gambling dens where they would be cheated by the "big mitt" men.

man." Roman Meix alone had the distinction among all the Minneapolis victims of going by his own name. Having lost $775, he became known for his persistent complainings. But they all "kicked" some. To Norbeck at the street door was assigned the duty of hearing their complaints, and "throwing a scare into them." "Oh, so you've been gambling," he would say. "Have you got a license? Well, then, you better get right out of this town." Sometimes he accompanied them to the station and saw them off. If they were not to be put off thus, he directed them to the chief of police. Fred Ames tried to wear them out by keeping them waiting in the anteroom. If they outlasted him, he saw them and frightened them with threats of all sorts of trouble for gambling without a license. Meix wanted to have payment on his check stopped. Ames, who had been a bank clerk, told him so, and then had the effrontery to say that payment on such a check could not be stopped.

Burglaries were common. How many the police planned may never be known. Charles F. Brackett and Fred Malone, police captains and detectives, were active, and one well-established crime of theirs is the robbery of the Pabst Brewing Company office. They persuaded two men, one an employee, to learn the combination of the safe, open and clean it out one night, while the two officers stood guard outside.

The excesses of the municipal administration became so notorious that some of the members of it remonstrated with the others, and certain county officers were genuinely alarmed. No restraint followed their warnings. Sheriff Megaarden, no Puritan himself, felt constrained to interfere, and he made some arrests of gamblers. The Ames people turned upon him in a fury; they accused him of making overcharges in his accounts with the county for fees, and laying the evidence before Governor Van Sant, they had Megaarden removed from office. Ames offered bribes to two county commissioners to appoint Gardner sheriff, so as to be sure of no more trouble in that quarter. This move failed, but the lesson taught Megaarden served to clear the atmosphere, and the spoliation went on as recklessly as ever. It became impossible.

Even lawlessness must be regulated. Dr. Ames, never an organizer, attempted no control, and his followers began to quarrel among themselves. They deceived one another; they robbed the thieves; they robbed Ames himself. His brother became dissatisfied with his share of the spoils, and formed cabals with captains who plotted against the administration and set up disorderly houses, "panel games," and all sorts of "grafts" of their own. The one man loyal to the mayor was Gardner, and Fred Ames, Captain King, and their pals, plotted the fall of the favorite. Now anybody could get anything from the Doctor, if he could have him alone. The Fred Ames clique chose a time when the mayor was at West Baden; they filled him with suspicion of Gardner and the fear of exposure, and induced him to let a creature named

"Reddy" Cohen, instead of Gardner, do the collecting, and pay over all the moneys, not directly, but through Fred. Gardner made a touching appeal. "I have been honest. I have paid you all," he said to the mayor. "Fred and the rest will rob you." This was true, but it was of no avail.

Fred Ames was in charge at last, and he himself went about giving notice of the change. Three detectives were with him when he visited the women, and here is the women's story, in the words of one, as it was told again and again in court: "Colonel Ames came in with the detectives. He stepped into a side room and asked me if I had been paying Gardner. I told him I had, and he told me not to pay no more, but to come to his office later, and he would let me know what to do. I went to the City Hall in about three weeks, after Cohen had called and said he was 'the party.' I asked the chief if it was all right to pay Cohen, and he said it was."

The new arrangement did not work so smoothly as the old. Cohen was an oppressive collector, and Fred Ames, appealed to, was weak and lenient. He had no sure hold on the force. His captains, free of Gardner, were undermining the chief. They increased their private operations. Some of the detectives began to drink hard and neglect their work. Norbeck so worried the "big mitt" men by staying away from the joint, that they complained to Fred about him. The chief rebuked Norbeck, and he promised to "do better," but thereafter he was paid, not by the week, but by piece work—so much for each "trimmed sucker" that he ran out of town. Protected swindlers were arrested for operating in the street by "Coffee John's" new policemen who took the places of the negligent detectives. Fred let the indignant prisoners go when they were brought before him, but the arrests were annoying, inconvenient, and disturbed business. The whole system became so demoralized that every man was for himself. There was not left even the traditional honor among thieves.

It was at this juncture, in April, 1902, that the grand jury for the summer term was drawn. An ordinary body of unselected citizens, it received no special instructions from the bench; the county prosecutor offered it only routine work to do. But there was a man among them who was a fighter—the foreman, Hovey C. Clarke. He was of an old New England family. Coming to Minneapolis when a young man, seventeen years before, he had fought for employment, fought with his employers for position, fought with his employees, the lumber-Jacks, for command, fought for his company against competitors; and he had won always, till now he had the habit of command, the impatient, imperious manner of the master, and the assurance of success which begets it. He did not want to be a grand juryman, he did not want to be a foreman; but since he was both, he wanted to accomplish something.

Why not rip up the Ames gang? Heads shook, hands went up; it was useless to try. The discouragement fired Clarke. That was just what he would do, he said, and he took stock of his jury. Two or three were men with backbone; that he knew, and he quickly had them with him. The rest were all sorts of men. Mr. Clarke won over each man to himself, and interested them all. Then he called for the county prosecutor. The prosecutor was a politician; he knew the Ames crowd; they were too powerful to attack.

"You are excused," said the foreman.

There was a scene; the prosecutor knew his rights.

"Do you think, Mr. Clarke," he cried, "that you can run the grand jury and my office, too?"

"Yes," said Clarke, "I will run your office if I want to; and I want to. You're excused."

Mr. Clarke does not talk much about his doings last summer; he isn't the talking sort. But he does say that all he did was to apply simple business methods to his problem. In action, however, these turned out to be the most approved police methods. He hired a lot of local detectives who, he knew, would talk about what they were doing, and thus would be watched by the police. Having thus thrown a false scent, he hired some other detectives whom nobody knew about. This was expensive; so were many of the other things he did; but he was bound to win, so he paid the price, drawing freely on his own and his colleagues' pockets. (The total cost to the county for a long summer's work by this grand jury was $259.) With his detectives out, he himself went to the jail to get tips from the inside, from criminals who, being there, must have grievances. He made the acquaintance of the jailor, Captain Alexander, and Alexander was a friend of Sheriff Megaarden. Yes, he had some men there who were "sore" and might want to get even.

Now two of these were "big mitt" men who had worked for Gardner. One was "Billy" Edwards, the other "Cheerful Charlie" Howard. I heard too many explanations of their plight to choose any one; this general account will cover the ground: In the Ames mêlée, either by mistake, neglect, or for spite growing out of the network of conflicting interests and gangs, they were arrested, arraigned, not before Fred Ames, but a judge, and held in bail too high for them to furnish. They had paid for an unexpired period of protection, yet could get neither protection nor bail. They were forgotten. "We got the double cross all right," they said, and they bled with their grievance; but squeal, no, sir!—that was "another deal."

But Mr. Clarke had their story, and he was bound to force them to tell it under oath on the stand. If they did, Gardner and Norbeck would be indicted, tried, and probably convicted. In themselves, these men were of no great importance; but they were the key to the situation, and a way up to the mayor.

It was worth trying. Mr. Clarke went into the jail with Messrs. Lester Elwood and Willard J. Hield, grand jurors on whom he relied most for delicate work. They stood by while the foreman talked. And the foreman's way of talking was to smile, swear, threaten, and cajole. "Billy" Edwards told me afterwards that he and Howard were finally persuaded to turn state's evidence, because they believed that Mr. Clarke was the kind of a man to keep his promises and fulfil his threats, "We," he said, meaning criminals generally, "are always stacking up against juries and lawyers who want us to holler. We don't, because we see they ain't wise, and won't get there. They're quitters; they can be pulled off. Clarke has a hard eye. I know men. It's my business to size 'em up, and I took him for a winner, and I played in with him against that whole big bunch of easy things that was running things on the bum." The grand jury was ready at the end of three weeks of hard work to find bills. A prosecutor was needed. The public prosecutor was being ignored, but his first assistant and friend, Al. J. Smith, was taken in hand by Mr. Clarke. Smith hesitated; he knew better even than the foreman the power and resources of the Ames gang. But he came to believe in Mr. Clarke, just as Edwards had; he was sure the foreman would win; so he went over to his side, and, having once decided, he led the open fighting, and, alone in court, won cases against men who had the best lawyers in the State to defend them. His court record is extraordinary. Moreover, he took over the negotiations with criminals for evidence, Messrs. Clarke, Hield, Elwood, and the other jurors providing means and moral support. These were needed. Bribes were offered to Smith; he was threatened; he was called a fool. But so was Clarke, to whom $28,000 was offered to quit, and for whose slaughter a slugger was hired to come from Chicago. What startled the jury most, however, was the character of the citizens who were sent to them to dissuade them from their course. No reform I ever studied has failed to bring out this phenomenon of virtuous cowardice, the baseness of the decent citizen.

Nothing stopped this jury, however. They had courage. They indicted Gardner, Norbeck, Fred Ames, and many lesser persons. But the gang had courage, too, and raised a defence fund to fight Clarke. Mayor Ames was defiant. Once, when Mr. Clarke called at the City Hall, the mayor met and challenged him. The mayor's heelers were all about him, but Clarke faced him.

"Yes, Doc. Ames, I'm after you," he said. "I've been in this town for seventeen years, and all that time you've been a moral leper. I hear you were rotten during the ten years before that. Now I'm going to put you where all contagious things are put—where you cannot contaminate anybody else."

The trial of Gardner came on. Efforts had been made to persuade him to surrender the mayor, but the young man was paid $15,000 "to stand pat," and he went to trial and conviction silent. Other trials followed fast—Norbeck's, Fred Ames's, Chief of Detectives King's. Witnesses who were out of the State were needed, and true testimony from women. There was no county money for extradition, so the grand jurors paid these costs also. They had Meix followed from Michigan down to Mexico and back to Idaho, where they got him, and he was presented in court one day at the trial of Norbeck, who had "steered" him out of town. Norbeck thought Meix was a thousand miles away, and had been bold before. At the sight of him in court he started to his feet, and that night ran away. The jury spent more money in his pursuit, and they caught him. He confessed, but his evidence was not accepted. He was sentenced to three years in state's prison. Men caved all around, but the women were firm, and the first trial of Fred Ames failed. To break the women's faith in the ring, Mayor Ames was indicted for offering the bribe to have Gardner made sheriff—a genuine, but not the best case against him. It brought the women down to the truth, and Fred Ames, retried, was convicted and sentenced to six and a half years in state's prison. King was tried for accessory to felony (helping in the theft of a diamond, which he afterward stole from the thieves), and sentenced to three and a half years in prison. And still the indictments came, with trials following fast. Al. Smith resigned with the consent and thanks of the grand jury; his chief, who was to run for the same office again, wanted to try the rest of the cases, and he did very well.

All men were now on the side of law and order. The panic among the "grafters" was laughable, in spite of its hideous significance. Two heads of departments against whom nothing had been shown suddenly ran away, and thus suggested to the grand jury an inquiry which revealed another source of "graft," in the sale of supplies to public institutions and the diversion of great quantities of provisions to the private residences of the mayor and other officials. Mayor Ames, under indictment and heavy bonds for extortion, conspiracy, and bribe-offering, left the State on a night train; a gentleman who knew him by sight saw him sitting up at eleven o'clock in the smoking-room of the sleeping-car, an unlighted cigar in his mouth, his face ashen and drawn, and at six o'clock the next morning he still was sitting there, his cigar still unlighted. He went to West Baden, a health resort in Indiana, a sick and broken man, aging years in a month. The city was without a mayor, the ring was without a leader; cliques ruled, and they pictured one another hanging about the grand-jury room begging leave to turn state's evidence. Tom Brown, the mayor's secretary, was in the mayor's chair; across the hall sat Fred Ames, the chief of police, balancing Brown's light weight. Both were busy forming cliques within the ring. Brown had on his side Coffee John and Police Captain Hill. Ames had Captain "Norm" King (though he had been convicted and had resigned), Captain Krumweide, and Ernest Wheelock, the chief's secretary. Alderman D. Percy Jones, the president of the council, an honorable man, should have taken the chair, but he was in the East; so this unstable equilibrium was all the city had by way of a government.

Then Fred Ames disappeared. The Tom Brown clique had full sway, and took over the police department. This was a shock to everybody, to none more than to the King clique, which joined in the search for Ames. An alderman, Fred M. Powers, who was to run for mayor on the Republican ticket, took charge of the mayor's office, but he was not sure of his authority or clear as to his policy. The grand jury was the real power behind him, and the foreman was telegraphing for Alderman Jones. Meanwhile the cliques were making appeals to Mayor Ames, in West Baden, and each side that saw him received authority to do its will. The Coffee John clique, denied admission to the grand-jury room, turned to Alderman Powers, and were beginning to feel secure, when they heard that Fred Ames was coming back. They rushed around, and obtained an assurance from the exiled mayor that Fred was returning only to resign. Fred—now under conviction—returned, but he did not resign; supported by his friends, he took charge again of the police force. Coffee John besought Alderman Powers to remove the chief, and when the acting mayor proved himself too timid, Coffee John, Tom Brown, and Captain Hill laid a deep plot. They would ask Mayor Ames to remove his brother. This they felt sure they could persuade the "old man" to do. The difficulty was to keep him from changing his mind when the other side should reach his ear. They hit upon a bold expedient. They would urge the "old man" to remove Fred, and then resign himself, so that he could not undo the deed that they wanted done. Coffee John and Captain Hill slipped out of town one night; they reached West Baden on one train and they left for home on the next, with a demand for Fred's resignation in one hand and the mayor's own in the other. Fred Ames did resign, and though the mayor's resignation was laid aside for a while, to avoid the expense of a special election, all looked well for Coffee John and his clique. They had Fred out, and Alderman Powers was to make them great. But Mr. Powers wobbled. No doubt the grand jury spoke to him. At any rate he turned most unexpectedly on both cliques together. He turned out Tom Brown, but he turned out also Coffee John, and he did not make their man chief of police, but another of some one else's selection. A number of resignations was the result, and these the acting mayor accepted, making a clearing of astonished rascals which was very gratifying to the grand jury and to the nervous citizens of Minneapolis.

But the town was not yet easy. The grand jury, which was the actual head of the government, was about to be discharged, and, besides, their work was destructive. A constructive force was now needed, and Alderman Jones was pelted with telegrams from home bidding him hurry back. He did hurry, and when he arrived, the situation was instantly in control. The grand jury prepared to report, for the city had a mind and a will of its own once more. The criminals found it out last.

Percy Jones, as his friends call him, is of the second generation of his family in Minneapolis. His father started him well-to-do, and he went on from where he was started. College graduate and business man, he has a conscience which, however, he has brains enough to question. He is not the fighter, but the slow, sure executive. As an alderman he is the result of a movement begun several years ago by some young men who were convinced by an exposure of a corrupt municipal council that they should go into politics. A few did go in; Jones was one of these few.

The acting mayor was confronted at once with all the hardest problems of municipal government. Vice rose right up to tempt or to fight him. He studied the situation deliberately, and by and by began to settle it point by point, slowly but finally, against all sorts of opposition. One of his first acts was to remove all the proved rascals on the force, putting in their places men who had been removed by Mayor Ames. Another important step was the appointment of a church deacon and personal friend to be chief of police, this on the theory that he wanted at the head of his police a man who could have no sympathy with crime, a man whom he could implicitly trust. Disorderly houses, forbidden by law, were permitted, but only within certain patrol lines, and they were to pay nothing, in either blackmail or "fines." The number and the standing and the point of view of the "good people" who opposed this order was a lesson to Mr. Jones in practical government. One very prominent citizen and church member threatened him for driving women out of two flats owned by him; the rent was the surest means of "support for his wife and children." Mr. Jones enforced his order.

Other interests—saloon-keepers, brewers, etc.—gave him trouble enough, but all these were trifles in comparison with his experience with the gamblers. They represented organized crime, and they asked for a hearing. Mr. Jones gave them some six weeks for negotiations. They proposed a solution. They said that if he would let them (a syndicate) open four gambling places down town, they would see that no others ran in any part of the city. Mr. Jones pondered and shook his head, drawing them on. They went away, and came back with a better promise. Though they were not the associates of criminals, they knew that class and their plans. No honest police force, unaided, could deal with crime. Thieves would soon be at work again, and what could Mr. Jones do against them with a police force headed by a church deacon? The gamblers offered to control the criminals for the city.

Mr. Jones, deeply interested, declared he did not believe there was any danger of fresh crimes. The gamblers smiled and went away. By an odd coincidence there happened just after that what the papers called "an epidemic of crime." They were petty thefts, but they occupied the mind of the acting mayor. He wondered at their opportuneness. He wondered how the news of them got out.

The gamblers soon reappeared. Hadn't they told Mr. Jones crime would soon be prevalent in town again? They had, indeed, but the mayor was unmoved; "porch climbers" could not frighten him. But this was only the beginning, the gamblers said: the larger crimes would come next. And they went away again. Sure enough, the large crimes came. One, two, three burglaries of jewelry in the houses of well-known people occurred; then there was a fourth, and the fourth was in the house of a relative of the acting mayor. He was seriously amused. The papers had the news promptly, and not from the police.

The gamblers called again. If they could have the exclusive control of gambling in Minneapolis, they would do all that they had promised before, and, if any large burglaries occurred, they would undertake to recover the "swag," and sometimes catch the thief. Mr. Jones was sceptical of their ability to do all this. The gamblers offered to prove it. How? They would get back for Mr. Jones the jewelry recently reported stolen from four houses in town. Mr. Jones expressed a curiosity to see this done, and the gamblers went away. After a few days the stolen jewelry, parcel by parcel, began to return; with all due police-criminal mystery it was delivered to the chief of police.

When the gamblers called again, they found the acting mayor ready to give his decision on their propositions. It was this: There should be no gambling, with police connivance, in the city of Minneapolis during his term of office.

Mr. Jones told me that if he had before him a long term, he certainly would reconsider this answer. He believed he would decide again as he had already, but he would at least give studious reflection to the question—Can a city be governed without any alliance with crime? It was an open question. He had closed it only for the four months of his emergency administration. Minneapolis should be clean and sweet for a little while at least, and the new administration should begin with a clear deck.

EDITOR'S NOTE—The people of Minneapolis rose to the emergency on Election Day, November 4th. Though for all other offices they elected a straight Republican ticket, for Mayor they preferred James C. Haynes, the Democratic candidate, to "Alderman" Powers (Rep.) by some 6,000 majority. Clarke and Jones both refused to run.

IDA M. TARBELL

The Oil War of 1872

Chapter III of the History
of the Standard Oil Company

"The Oil War of 1872" was Ida Tarbell's third essay on the history of the Standard Oil Company. The article tells the story of a bitter conflict that arose among Pennsylvania oil producers and the South Improvement Company. As Tarbell explains, the head of the Standard Oil Company, John D. Rockefeller, and his associates conspired with the railroads to set favorable rates for a few large refiners at the expense of independent oil producers. The result was a ferocious battle in the oil regions for control of the fledgling but immensely profitable industry. (See page 27 of the Introduction for some questions raised by Tarbell's history.)

For several days an uneasy rumor had been running up and down the Oil Regions. Freight rates were going up. Now an advance in a man's freight bill may ruin his business; more, it may mean the ruin of a region. Rumor said that the new rate meant just this; that is, that it more than covered the margin of profit in any branch of the oil business. There was another feature to the report; the railroads were not going to apply the proposed tariffs to everybody. They had agreed to give to a company unheard of until now—the South Improvement Company—a special rate considerably lower than the new open rate. It was only a rumor and many people discredited it. *Why* should the railroads ruin the Oil Regions to build up a company of outsiders?

THE UPRISING IN THE OIL REGIONS

On the morning of February 26, 1872, the oil men read in their morning papers that the rise which had been threatening had come; moreover, that all members of the South Improvement Company were exempt from the advance. At the news all Oildom rushed into the streets. Nobody waited to find out his neighbor's opinion. On every lip there was but one word, and that was "conspiracy." In the vernacular of the region, it was evident that "a torpedo was filling for that scheme."

In twenty-four hours after the announcement of the increase in freight rates a mass meeting of three thousand excited, gesticulating oil men was gathered in the Opera House at Titusville. Producers, brokers, refiners, drillers, pumpers were in the crowd. Their temper was shown by the mottoes on the banners which they carried: "Down with the conspirators"—"No compromise"—"Don't give up the ship!" Three days later, as large a meeting was held at Oil City, its temper more warlike if possible; and so it went. They organized a Petroleum Producers' Union, pledged themselves to reduce their production by starting no new wells for sixty days and by shutting down on Sundays, to sell no oil to any person known to be in the South Improvement Company, but to support the Creek refiners and those elsewhere who had refused to go into the combination, to boycott the offending railroads, and to build lines which they would own and control themselves. They sent a committee to the Legislature asking that the charter of the South Improvement Company be repealed, and another to Congress demanding an investigation of the whole business on the ground that it was an interference with trade. They ordered that a history of the conspiracy, giving the names of the conspirators and the designs of the company, should be prepared, and 30,000 copies sent to "judges of all courts, Senators of the United States, members of Congress and of State Legislatures, and to all railroad men and prominent business men of the country, *to the end that enemies of the freedom of trade may be known and shunned by all honest men.*"

They prepared a petition ninety-three feet long, praying for a free pipe-line bill, something which they had long wanted, but which, so far, the Pennsylvania Railroad had prevented their getting, and sent it by a committee to the Legislature; and for days they kept a thousand men ready to march on Harrisburg at a moment's notice if the Legislature showed signs of refusing their demands. In short, for weeks the whole body of oil men abandoned regular business and surged from town to town intent on destroying the "Monster," the "Forty Thieves," the "Great Anaconda," as they called the mysterious South Improvement Company. Curiously enough, it was chiefly against the combination which had secured the discrimination from the railroads—not the railroads which had granted it—that their fury was directed. They expected nothing but robbery from the railroads, they said. They were used to that; but they would not endure it from men in their own business.

FIGHTING IN THE DARK

When they began the fight, the mass of the oil men knew nothing more of the South Improvement Company than its name and the fact that it had secured

from the railroads advantages in rates which were bound to ruin all independent refiners of oil and to put all producers at its mercy. Their tempers
were not improved by the discovery that it was a secret organization, and
had been at work under their very eyes for some weeks without their know-
ing it. At the first public meeting this fact came out, leading refiners of the
Region relating their experience with the "Anaconda." According to one of
these gentlemen, Mr. J. D. Archbold—the same who afterward became vice-
president of the Standard Oil Company, which office he now holds—he and
his partners had heard of the scheme some months before. Alarmed by the
rumor, a committee of independent refiners had attempted to investigate, but
could learn nothing until they had given a promise not to reveal what was told
them. When convinced that a company had been formed actually strong
enough to force or persuade the railroads to give to it special rates and refuse
them to all persons outside, Mr. Archbold said that he and his colleagues had
gone to the railway kings to remonstrate, but all to no effect. The South
Improvement Company by some means had convinced the railroads that they
owned the Oil Regions, producers and refiners both, and that hereafter no oil
of any account would be shipped except as they shipped it. Mr. Archbold and
his partners had been asked to join the company, but had refused, declaring
that the whole business was iniquitous, that they would fight it to the end,
and that in their fight they would have the backing of the oil men, as a whole.
They excused their silence up to this time by citing the pledge exacted from
them before they were informed of the extent and nature of the South
Improvement Company.

THE "DERRICK'S" BLACKLIST

Naturally the burning question throughout the Oil Region, convinced as it was
of the iniquity of the scheme, was: who are the conspirators? Whether the
gentlemen concerned regarded themselves in the light of "conspirators" or not,
they seem from the first to have realized that it would be discreet not to be
identified publicly with the scheme, and to have allowed one name alone to
appear in all signed negotiations. This was the name of the president, Peter
H. Watson. However anxious the members of the South Improvement Company were that Mr. Watson should combine the honors of president with the
trials of scapegoat, it was impossible to keep their names concealed. The Oil
City Derrick, at that time one of the most vigorous, witty, and daring newspapers in the country, began a blacklist at the head of its editorial columns the
day after the raise in freights was announced, and it kept it there until it was
believed complete. It stood finally as follows:

THE BLACK LIST

P. H. WATSON, PRES. S. I. CO.

Charles Lockhart,

W. P. Logan,

R. S. Waring,

A. W. Bostwick,

W. G. Warden,

John Rockefeller,

Amasa Stone.

These seven are given as the
Directors of the Southern Improvement Company.
They are refiners or merchants of petroleum

Atlantic & Gt. Western Railway.

L. S. & M. S. Railway.

Philadelphia & Eric Railway.

Pennsylvania Central Railway.

New York Central Railway.

Erie Railway.

Behold "The Anaconda" in all his hideous deformity!

This list was not exact,* but it was enough to go on, and the oil blockade, to which the Petroleum Producer's Union had pledged itself, was now enforced against the firms listed, and as far as possible against the railroads. All of these refineries had their buyers on the Creek, and although several of the buyers were young men generally liked for their personal and business qualities, no mercy was shown them. They were refused oil by everybody, though they offered from seventy-five cents to a dollar more than the market price. They were ordered at one meeting "to desist from their nefarious business or leave the Oil Region," and when they declined they were invited to resign from the Oil Exchanges of which they were members. So strictly, indeed, was the blockade enforced that in Cleveland the refineries were closed

*See *McClure's Magazine* for December 1902 for stockholders of the South Improvement Company and list of railroads signing contracts with the Company.

and meetings for the relief of the workmen were held. In spite of the excitement there was little vandalism, the only violence at the opening of the war being at Franklin, where a quantity of the oil belonging to Mr. Watson was run on the ground.

THE OIL MEN ASK LEADING QUESTIONS

The sudden uprising of the Oil Regions against the South Improvement Company did not alarm its members at first. The excitement would die out, they told one another. All that they needed to do was to keep quiet, and stay out of the oil country. But the excitement did not die out. Indeed, with every day it became more intense and more widespread. When Mr. Watson's tanks were tapped he began to protest in letters to a friend, F. W. Mitchell, a prominent banker and oil man of Franklin. The company was misunderstood, he complained. "Have a committee of leading producers appointed," he wrote, and "we will show that the contracts with the railroad are as favorable to the producing as to other interests; that the much-denounced rebate will enhance the price of oil at the wells, and that our entire plan in operation and effect will promote every legitimate American interest in the oil trade." Mr. Mitchell urged Mr. Watson to come openly to the Oil Regions and meet the producers as a body. A mass meeting was never a "deliberative body," Mr. Watson replied, but if a few of the leading oil men would go to Albany or New York, or any place favorable to calm investigation and deliberation, and therefore outside of the atmosphere of excitement which enveloped the Oil Country, he would see them. These letters were read to the producers, and a motion to appoint a committee was made. It was received with protests and jeers. Mr. Watson was afraid to come to the Oil Regions, they said. The letters were not addressed to the association, they were private—an insult to the body. "We are lowering our dignity to treat with this man Watson," declared one man. "He is free to come to these meetings if he wants to." "What is there to negotiate about?" asked another. "To open a negotiation is to concede that we are wrong. Can we go halves with these middlemen in their swindle?" "He has set a trap for us," declared another. "We cannot treat with him without guilt," and the motion was voted down.

The stopping of the oil supply finally forced the South Improvement Company to recognize the Producers' Union officially, by asking that a committee of the body be appointed to confer with them, on a compromise. The producers sent back a pertinent answer. They believed the South Improvement Company meant to monopolize the oil business. If that was so they could not consider a compromise with it. If they were wrong, they would be glad to be enlightened, and they asked for information. First: the charter under which the South Improvement Company was organized. Second: the articles of association. Third: the officers' names. Fourth: the contracts with the railroads and who signed them. Fifth: the general plan of management.

Until we know these things, the oil men declared, we can no more negotiate with you than we could sit down to negotiate with a burglar as to his privileges in our house.

AN OMNIBUS CHARTER

The Producers' Union did not get the information they asked from the company at that time, but it was not long before they did, and much more, too. The committee which they had appointed to write a history of the South Improvement Company reported on March 20th, and in April the Congressional Committee appointed at the insistence of the oil men made its investigation. The former report was published broadcast, and is readily accessible to-day. The Congressional investigation was not published officially, and no trace of its work can now be found in Washington, but while it was going on, reports were made in the newspapers of the Oil Regions, and at its close the Producers' Union published in Lancaster, Pennsylvania, a pamphlet called the "Rise and Fall of the South Improvement Company," which contains the full testimony taken by the committee. This pamphlet is rare, the writer never having been able to find a copy save in three or four private collections. The most important part of it is the testimony of Peter H. Watson, the president, and W. G. Warden, the secretary of the South Improvement Company. It was in these documents that the oil men found full justification for the war they were carrying on and for the losses they had caused themselves and others. Nothing, indeed, could have been more damaging to a corporation than the publication of the charter of the South Improvement Company. As its president told the Congressional Investigating Committee, when he was under examination, "this charter was a sort of clothes-horse to hang a scheme upon." As a matter of fact, it was a clothes-horse big enough to hang the earth upon. It granted powers practically unlimited. There really was no exaggeration in the summary of its powers made and scattered broadcast by the irate oil men in their "History of the South Improvement Company":

> The Southern Improvement Company can own, contract or operate any work, business or traffic (save only banking); may hold and transfer any kind of property, real or personal; hold and operate on any leased property (oil territory, for instance); make any kind of contract; deal in stocks, securities, and funds: loan its credit; guarantee any one's paper; manipulate

any industry; may seize upon the lands of other parties for railroading or *any other purpose;* may absorb the improvements, property or franchises of any other company, *ad infinitum;* may fix the fares, tolls or freights to be charged on lines of transit operated by it, or on any business it gives to *any other company* or line, without limit.

Its capital stock can be expanded or "watered" at liberty; it can change its name and location at pleasure; can go anywhere and do almost anything. It is not a Pennsylvania corporation, only; it can, so far as these enactments are valid, or are confirmed by other Legislatures, operate in any State or Territory; its directors must be only citizens of the United States—not necessarily of Pennsylvania. It is responsible to no one; its stockholders are only liable to the amount of their stock in it; its directors, when wielding all the princely powers of the corporation, are also responsible only to the amount of their stock in it; it may control the business of the continent and hold and transfer millions of property and yet be rotten to the core. It is responsible to no one; makes no reports of its acts or financial condition; its records and deliberations are secret; its capital illimitable; its object unknown. It can be here to-day, to-morrow away. Its domain is the whole country, its business everything. Now it is petroleum it grasps and monopolizes; next year it may be iron, coal, cotton, or breadstuffs. They are landsmen granted perpetual letters of marque to prey upon all commerce everywhere.

When the course of this charter through the Pennsylvania Legislature came to be traced, it was found to be devious and uncertain. The company had been incorporated in 1870, and vested with all the "powers, privileges, duties, and obligations" of two earlier companies—the Continental Improvement Company and the Pennsylvania Company, both of which were children of that interesting body known as the "Tom Scott Legislature." The act incorporating the company was never published, the name of the member introducing it was never known, and no votes on it are recorded. The origin of the South Improvement Company has always remained in darkness. It was one of thirteen "improvement" companies chartered in Pennsylvania at about the same time, and enjoying the same commercial *carte blanche.*

AMAZING CONTRACTS WITH THE RAILROADS

Bad as the charter was in appearance, the oil men found that the contracts which the new company had made with the railroads were worse. These contracts advanced the rates of freight from the Oil Regions over 100 per cent., but it was not the railroad that got the greater part of this advance; it was the South Improvement Company. Not only did it ship its own oil at fully a dollar a barrel cheaper on an average than anybody else could, but it received fully a dollar a barrel "rake-off" on every barrel its competitors shipped. It was computed and admitted by the members of the company who appeared before the investigating committee of Congress that this discrimination would have turned over to them fully $6,000,000 annually on the carrying trade. It is hardly to be wondered at that when the oil men had before them the full text of these contracts they refused absolutely to accept the repeated assertions of the members of the South Improvement Company that their scheme was intended only for "the good of the oil business." The committee of Congress could not be persuaded to believe it either. "Your success meant the destruction of every refiner who refused for any reason to join your company, or whom you did not care to have in, and it put the producers entirely in your power. It would make a monopoly such as no set of men are fit to handle," the chairman of the committee declared. Mr. Warden, the secretary of the company, protested again and again that they meant to take in all the refiners, though he had to admit that the contracts with the railroads were not made on this condition. Mr. Watson affirmed and reaffirmed before the committee that it was the intention of the company to take care of the producers. "It was an essential part of this contract that the producers should join it," he declared. But no such condition was embodied in the contract. It was verbal only, and, besides, it had never been submitted to the producers themselves in any form until after the trouble in the Oil Region began. The committee, like the oil men, insisted that under the circumstances no such verbal understanding was to be trusted.

No part of the testimony before the committee made a worse impression than that showing that one of the chief objects of the combination was to put up the price of refined oil. "Under your arrangement," said the chairman, "the public would have been put to an additional expense of $7,500,000 a year." "What public?" said Mr. Warden. "They would have had to pay it in Europe." "But to keep up the price abroad you would have to keep up the price at home," said the chairman. Mr. Warden conceded the point: "You could not get a better price for that exported without having a better price here." Thirty-two cents a gallon was the ideal price they had in view, though refined had not sold for that since 1869, the average price in 1870 being 26⅜ and in 1871 24¼. The average price of crude in 1870 was $3.90 a barrel; in 1871, $4.40. The Congressional Committee claimed that any combination formed for the purpose of putting up the price of an article of general consumption was an injury to the public, but the members of the company would not admit it as such. Everybody in the business should make more money, they argued; the profits were too small—the consumer ought to be willing to pay more.

POPULAR SYMPATHY FOR THE OIL REGIONS

It did not take the full exposition of the objects of the South Improvement Company, brought out by the Congressional Investigating Committee, with the publication of charters and contracts, to convince the country at large that the Oil Regions were right in their opposition. From the first the sympathy of the press and the people were with the oil men. It was evident to everybody that if the railroads had made the contracts as charged (and it daily became more evident they had done so), nothing but an absolute monopoly of the whole oil business by this combination could result. It was robbery, cried the newspapers all over the land. "Under the thin guise of assisting in the development of oil refining in Pittsburg and Cleveland," said the New York *Tribune*, "this corporation has simply laid its hand upon the throat of the oil traffic with a demand to 'stand and deliver.'" And if this could be done in the oil business, what was to prevent its being done in any other industry? Why should not a company be formed to control wheat or beef or iron or steel, as well as oil? If the railroads would do this for one company, why not for another? The South Improvement Company, men agreed, was a menace to the free trade of the country. If the oil men yielded now, all industries must suffer from their weakness. The railroads must be taught a lesson as well as would-be monopolists.

REINFORCEMENTS FROM NEW YORK

The oil men had no thought of yielding. With every day of the war their backbones grew stiffer. The men were calmer, too, for their resistance had found a moral ground which seemed impregnable to them, and arguments against the South Improvement Company now took the place of denunciations. The country so buzzed with discussion on the duties of the railroads, that reporters sent from the Eastern newspapers commented on it. Nothing was commoner, indeed, on the trains which ran the length of the region, and were its real forums, than to hear a man explaining that the railways derived their existence and power from the people, that their charters were contracts with the people, that a fundamental provision of these contracts was that there should be no discriminating in favor of one person or one town, that such a discrimination was a violation of charter, that therefore the South Improvement Company was founded on fraud, and the courts must dissolve it if the railways did not abandon it.

They now met the very plausible reasons given by the members of the company for their combination more intelligently than at first. There were grave abuses in the business, they admitted; there was too great refining capacity; but this they argued was a natural development in a new business whose growth had been extraordinary and whose limits were by no means defined. Time and experience would regulate it. Give the refiners open and regular freights, with no favors to any one, and the stronger and better equipped would live, the others die—but give all a chance. In fact, time and energy would regulate all the evils of which they complained if there was fair play.

The oil men were not only encouraged by public opinion and by getting their minds clear on the merits of their case; they were upheld by repeated proofs of aid from all sides; even the women of the region were asking what they could do, and offering to wear their "black velvet bonnets" all summer if necessary. Solid support came from the independent refiners and shippers in other parts of the country, who were offering to stand in with them in their contest. New York was already one of the chief refining centers of the country, and the South Improvement Company had left it entirely out of its combination. As incensed as the Creek itself, the New York interests formed an association, and about the middle of March sent a committee of three, with H. H. Rogers of Charles Pratt & Company at its head, to Oil City, to consult with the Producers' Union. Their arrival in the Oil Regions was a matter of great satisfaction. What made the oil men most exultant, however, was their growing belief that the railroads—the crux of the whole scheme—were weakening.

THE RAILROADS BACK DOWN

However fair the great scheme may have appeared to the railroad kings in the privacy of the council chamber, it began to look dark as soon as it was dragged into the open, and signs of a scuttle soon appeared. General G. B. McClellan, president of the Atlantic and Great Western, sent to the very first mass meeting this telegram:

> New York, February 27, 1872
> Neither the Atlantic and Great Western, or any of its officers, are interested in the South Improvement Company. Of course, the policy of the road is to accommodate the petroleum interest.   G. B. McClellan

A great applause was started, only to be stopped by the hisses of a group whose spokesman read the following:

> Contract with South Improvement Company signed by Geo. B. McClellan, president, for the Atlantic and Great Western Railroad. I only signed it after it was signed by all the other parties.   Jay Gould

The railroads tried in various ways to appease the oil men. They did not enforce the new rates. They had signed the contracts, they declared, only after the South Improvement Company had assured them that all the refineries and producers were to be taken in. Indeed, they seem to have realized within a fortnight that the scheme was doomed, and to have been quite ready to meet cordially a committee of oil men which went east to demand that the railroads revoke their contracts with the South Improvement Company. This committee, which was composed of twelve persons, three of them being the New York representatives already mentioned, began its work by an interview with Colonel Scott at the Colonial Hotel in Philadelphia. With evident pride the committee wrote back to the Producers' Union that: "Mr. Scott, differing in this respect from the railroad representatives whom we afterwards met, notified us that he would call upon us at our hotel." An interesting account of their interview was given to the Hepburn Committee in 1879 by Mr. W. T. Scheide, one of the number:

> We saw Mr. Scott on the 18th of March, 1872, in Philadelphia, and he said to us that he was very much surprised to hear of this agitation in the Oil Regions; that the object of the railroads in making this contract with the South Improvement Company was to obtain an evener to pool the freight— pool the oil freights among the different roads; that they had been cutting each other on oil freights for a number of years, and had not made any money out of it, although it was a freight they should have made money from; that they had endeavored to make an arrangement among themselves, but had always failed; he said that they supposed that the gentlemen representing the South Improvement Company represented the petroleum trade, but as he was now convinced they did not, he would be very glad to make an arrangement with this committee, who undoubtedly did represent the petroleum trade; the committee told him that they could not make any such contract; that they had no legal authority to do so; he said that could be easily fixed, because the Legislature was then in session, and by going to Harrisburg a charter could be obtained in a very few days; the committee still said that they would not agree to any such arrangement, that they did not think the South Improvement Company's contract was a good one, and they were instructed to have it broken, and so they did not feel that they could accept a similar one, even if they had the power.

Leaving Colonel Scott, the committee went on to New York, where they stayed for about a week, closely watched by the newspapers, all of which treated the "Oil War" as a national affair. Various conferences were held, leading up to a final all-important one on March 25th, at the Erie offices. Horace Clark, president of the Lake Shore and Michigan Southern Railroad, was chairman of this meeting, and, according to H. H. Rogers's testimony before the Hepburn Committee, in 1879, there were present, besides the oil men, Colonel Scott, General McClellan, Director Diven, William H. Vanderbilt, Mr. Stebbins, and George Hall.

MR. ROCKEFELLER TO THE RESCUE

The meeting had not been long in session before Mr. Watson, president of the South Improvement Company, and Mr. John D. Rockefeller, presented themselves for admission. Up to this time Mr. Rockefeller had kept well out of sight in the affair. He had given no interviews, offered no explanations. He had allowed the president of the company to wrestle with the excitement in his own way, but things were now in such critical shape that he came forward in a last attempt to save the organization by which he had been able to concentrate in his own hands the refining interests of Cleveland. With Mr. Watson, he knocked for admission to the council going on in the Erie offices. The oil men flatly refused to let them in. A dramatic scene followed, Mr. Clark, the chairman, protesting in agitated tones against shutting out his "life-long friend, Watson." The oil men were obdurate. They would have nothing to do with anybody concerned with the South Improvement Company. So determined were they that although Mr. Watson came in, he was obliged at once to withdraw. A *Times* reporter who witnessed the little scene between the two supporters of the tottering company after its president was turned out of the meeting remarks sympathetically that Mr. Rockefeller soon went away, "looking pretty blue."

The acquiescence of the "railroad kings" in the refusal of the oil men to recognize representatives of the South Improvement Company was followed by an unwilling promise to break the contracts with the company. A strong effort was made to persuade the independents to make the same contracts on condition that they shipped as much oil, but they would not hear of it. They demanded open rates, with no rebates to any one. The Vanderbilts particularly stuck for this arrangement, but were finally obliged to consent to revoke the contracts and to make a new one embodying the views of the Oil Regions. The contract finally signed at this meeting by H. F. Clark for the Lake Shore Road, O. H. P. Archer for the Erie, W. H. Vanderbilt for the Central, George B. McClellan for the Atlantic and Great Western, and Thomas A. Scott for the Pennsylvania, agreed that all shipping of oil should be made on "a basis of perfect equality to all shippers, producers, and refiners, and that no rebates, drawbacks, or other arrangements of any character shall be made or allowed that will give any party the slightest difference in rates or discriminations of any character whatever."

The same rate was put on refined oil from Cleveland, Pittsburg, and the

John D. Rockefeller
From a painting by Eastman Johnson

Creek, to eastern shipping points; that is, Mr. Rockefeller could send his oil from Cleveland to New York at $1.50 per barrel; so could his associates in Pittsburg, and this was what it cost the refiner on the Creek; but the latter had this advantage: he was at the wells. Mr. Rockefeller and his Pittsburg allies were miles away, and it cost them, by the new contract, fifty cents to get a barrel of crude to their works. The Oil Regions meant that geographical position should count. Unless there was some way to get around this contract, it looked at that moment very much as if Mr. Rockefeller had bought a white elephant when he swept up the refineries of Cleveland.

GRANT ON MONOPOLIES

This contract was the first effective thrust into the great bubble. Others followed in quick succession. On the 28th, the railroads officially annulled their contracts with the company. About the same time the Pennsylvania legislature repealed the charter. On March 30th, the committee of oil men sent to Washington to be present during the Congressional investigation, now about to begin, spent an hour with President Grant. They wired home that on their departure he said: "Gentlemen, I have noticed the progress of monopolies, and have long been convinced that the National Government would have to interfere and protect the people against them." The President and the members of Congress of both parties continued to show the greatest interest in the investigation, and there was little or no dissent from the final judgment of the committee, given early in May, that the South Improvement Company was the "most gigantic and daring conspiracy" a free country had ever seen. This decision finished the work. The "monster" was slain, the Oil Regions proclaimed exultantly.

THE STANDARD AGAIN BUYS OIL

And now came the question; what should they do about the blockade established against the members of the South Improvement Company? The railroads they had forgiven; should they forgive the members of the South Improvement Company? This question came up immediately on the repeal of the charter. The first severe test to which their temper was put was early in April, when a firm of Oil City brokers sold some 20,000 barrels of oil to the Standard Oil Company. The moment the sale was noised a perfect uproar burst forth. Indignant telegrams came from every direction condemning the brokers. "Betrayal," "infamy," "mercenary achievement," "the most unkindest cut of all," was the gist of them. From New York, Porter and Archbold telegraphed annulling all their contracts with the guilty brokers. The Oil Exchange passed votes of censure, and the Producers' Union turned them out. A few days later it was learned that a dealer on the Creek was preparing to ship 5,000 barrels to the same firm. A mob gathered about the cars and refused to let them leave. It was only by stationing a strong guard that the destruction of the oil was prevented.

But something had to be done. The cooler heads argued that the blockade, which had lasted now forty days, and from which the Region had, of course, suffered enormous loss, should be entirely lifted. The objects for which it had been established had been accomplished—that is, the South Improvement Company had been destroyed;—now let free trade be established. If anybody wanted to sell to "conspirators," it was his look-out. A long and excited meeting of men from the entire oil country was held at Oil City to discuss the question. At this meeting telegrams to the president of the Petroleum Producers' Union, Captain William Hasson, from officials of the railroads were read, declaring that the contracts with the South Improvement Company were canceled. Also the following from the Standard Oil Company was read:

Cleveland, Ohio, April 8, 1872
To Captain William Hasson: In answer to your telegram, this company holds no contract with the railroad companies or any of them, or with the South Improvement Company. The contracts between the South Improvement Company and the railroads have been canceled, and I am informed you have been so advised by telegram. I state unqualifiedly that reports circulated in the Oil Region and elsewhere, that this company, or any member of it, threatened to depress oil, are false.   John D. Rockefeller, President

It was finally decided that "inasmuch as the South Improvement Company contracts were annulled, and the Pennsylvania Legislature had taken pains to safeguard the interests of the trade, and Congress was moving on the same line, after the 15th trade should be free to all." This resolution put an official end to the "oil war."

But no number of resolutions could wipe out the memory of the forty days of terrible excitement and loss which the region had suffered. No triumph could stifle the suspicion and the bitterness which had been sown broadcast through the region. Every particle of independent manhood in these men whose very life was independent action had been outraged. Their sense of fair play, the saving force of the region in the days before law and order had been established, had been violated. These were things which could not be forgotten. There henceforth could be no trust in those who had devised a scheme which, the producers believed, was intended to rob them of their business.

THE SOUTH IMPROVEMENT COMPANY
ALIAS THE STANDARD OIL COMPANY

It was inevitable that under the pressure of their indignation and resentment some person or persons should be fixed upon as responsible, and should be hated accordingly. Before the lifting of the embargo this responsibility had been fixed. It was the Standard Oil Company of Cleveland, so the Oil Regions decided, which was at the bottom of the business, and the "Mephistopheles of the Cleveland Company," as they put it, was John D. Rockefeller. Even the

Cleveland *Herald* acknowledged this popular judgment. "Whether justly or unjustly," the editor wrote, "Cleveland has the odium of having originated the scheme." This opinion gained ground as the days passed. The activity of the president of the Standard in New York, in trying to save the contracts with the railroads, and his constant appearance with Mr. Watson, and the fact brought out by the Congressional investigation that a larger block of the South Improvement Company's stock was owned in the Standard than in any other firm, strengthened the belief. But what did more than anything else to fix the conviction was what they had learned of the career of the Standard Oil Company in Cleveland. Before the oil war the company had been known simply as one of several successful firms in that city. It drove close bargains, but it paid promptly, and was considered a desirable customer. Now the Oil Regions learned for the first time of the sudden and phenomenal expansion of the company. Where there had been at the beginning of 1872 twenty-six refining firms in Cleveland, there were but six left. In three months before and during the oil war the Standard had absorbed twenty plants. It was generally charged by the Cleveland refiners that Mr. Rockefeller had used the South Improvement scheme to persuade or compel his rivals to sell to him. "Why," cried the oil men, "the Standard Oil Company has done already in Cleveland what the South Improvement Company set out to do for the whole country, and it has done it by the same means."

By the time the blockade was raised, another unhappy conviction was fixed on the Oil Regions—the Standard Oil Company meant to carry out the plans of the exploded South Improvement Company. The promoters of the scheme were partly responsible for the report. Under the smart of their defeat they talked rather more freely than their policy of silence justified, and their remarks were quoted widely. Mr. Rockefeller was reported in the "Derrick" to have said to a prominent oil man of Oil City that the South Improvement Company could work under the charter of the Standard Oil Company, and to have predicted that in less than two months the gentleman would be glad to join him. The newspapers made much of the following similar story reported by a New York correspondent:

A prominent Cleveland member of what was the South Improvement Company had said within two days: The business *now* will be done by the Standard Oil Company. We have a rate of freight by water from Cleveland to New York at 70 cents. No man in the trade shall make a dollar this year. We purpose so manipulating the market as to run the price of crude on the Creek as low as two and a half. We mean to show the world that the South Improvement Company was organized for business and means business in spite of opposition. The same thing has been said in substance by the leading Philadelphia member.

Henry H. Rogers in 1872
Now president of the National Transit Company and a director of
the Standard Oil Company. The opposition to the South Improvement Company among the New York refiners was led by Mr. Rogers.

"The trade here regards the Standard Oil Company as simply taking the
place of the South Improvement Company and as being ready at any moment
to make the same attempt to control the trade as its progenitors did," said the
New York *Bulletin* about the middle of April. And the Cleveland *Herald*
discussed the situation under the heading, "South Improvement Company
alias Standard Oil Company." The effect of these reports in the Oil Regions
was most disastrous. Their open war became a kind of guerrilla opposition.
Those who sold oil to the Standard were ostracized, and its president was
openly scorned.

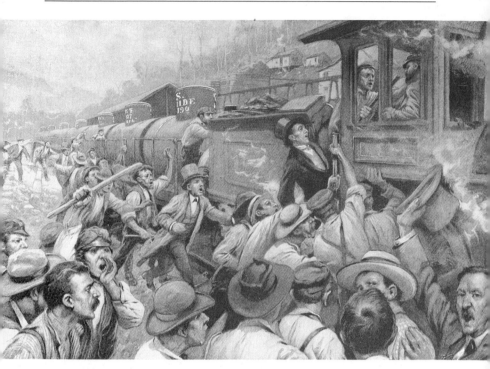

An Oil Riot   On April 9, 1872, it was learned that a train of tank cars on the siding at Rynd Farm, Oil Creek, was loading with oil for the Standard Oil Company of Cleveland. An excited crowd gathered, and prevented the train pulling out. The tanks and lines were guarded for some time.

MR. ROCKEFELLER BEGINS ALL OVER AGAIN

If Mr. Rockefeller had been an ordinary man the outburst of popular contempt and suspicion which suddenly poured on his head would have thwarted and crushed him. But he was no ordinary man. He had the powerful imagination to see what might be done with the oil business if it could be centered in his hands—the intelligence to analyze the problem into its elements and to find the key to control. He had the essential element to all great achievement, a steadfastness to a purpose once conceived which nothing can crush. The Oil Regions might rage, call him a conspirator and those who sold him oil traitors; the railroads might withdraw their contracts and the legislature annul his charter; undisturbed and unresting he kept at his great purpose. Even if his nature had not been such as to forbid him to abandon an enterprise in which he saw promise of vast profits, even if he had not had a mind which, stopped by a wall, burrows under or creeps around, he would nevertheless have been forced to desperate efforts to save his business. He had increased his refining capacity in Cleveland to 10,000 barrels on the strength of the South Improvement Company contracts. These contracts were annulled, and in their place was one signed by officials of all the oil-shipping roads refusing rebates to everybody. His geographical position was such that it cost him under these new contracts 50 cents more to get oil from the wells to New York than it did his rivals on the Creek. What could he do?

MR. ROCKEFELLER GETS A REBATE

He got a rebate. In spite of the binding nature of the contracts signed in New York on March 25th by representatives of all the railroads, before the middle of April the Standard Oil Company was shipping oil eastward from Cleveland for $1.25—this by the sworn testimony of Mr. H. M. Flagler before a commission of the Ohio State Legislature, in March, 1879. How much less a rate than $1.25 Mr. Rockefeller had before the end of April the writer does not know. Of course the rate was secret, and he probably understood now, as he had not two months before, how essential it was that he keep it secret. His task was more difficult now, for he had an enemy active, clamorous, contemptuous, whose suspicions had reached that acute point where they could believe nothing but evil of him—the producers and independents of the Oil Regions. It was utterly impossible that he should ever silence this enemy, for their points of view were diametrically opposed.

They believed in independent effort—every man for himself and fair play for all. They wanted competition, loved open fight. They considered that all business should be done openly—that the railways were bound as public carriers to give equal rates—that any combination which favored one firm or one locality at the expense of another was unjust and illegal.

MR. ROCKEFELLER'S OPINIONS AND CHARACTER

Mr. Rockefeller's point of view was different. He believed that the "good of all" was in a combination which would control the business as the South Improvement Company proposed to control it. Such a combination would end at once all the abuses the business suffered. As rebates and special rates were essential to this control, he favored them. Of course Mr. Rockefeller knew that the railroad was a public carrier, and that its charter forbade discrimination. But he knew that the railroads did not pretend to obey the laws governing them, that they regularly granted special rates and rebates to those who had large amounts of freight. That is, you could bargain with the railroads as you could with a man carrying on a strictly private business depending in no way on a public franchise. Moreover, Mr. Rockefeller knew that if he did not get rebates somebody else would; that they were for the wariest, the shrewdest, the most persistent. If somebody was to get rebates, why not he? This point of view was no uncommon one. Many men held it and felt a sort of scorn, as practical men always do for theorists, when it was contended that the shipper was as wrong in taking rates as the railroads in granting them.

Thus, on one hand there was an exaggerated sense of personal independence, on the other a firm belief in combination; on one hand a determination to root out the vicious system of rebates practised by the railway on the other a determination to keep it alive and profit by it. Those theories which the body of oil men held as vital and fundamental Mr. Rockefeller and his associates either did not comprehend or were deaf to. This lack of comprehension by many men of what seems to other men to be the most obvious principles of justice is not rare. Many men who are widely known as good, share it. Mr. Rockefeller was "good." There was no more faithful Baptist in Cleveland than he. Every enterprise of that church he had supported liberally from his youth. He gave to its poor. He visited its sick. He wept with its suffering. Moreover, he gave unostentatiously to many outside charities of whose worthiness he was satisfied. He was simple and frugal in his habits. He never went to the theater, never drank wine. He was a devoted husband, and he gave much time to the training of his children, seeking to develop in them his own habits of economy and of charity. Yet he was willing to strain every nerve to obtain for himself special and illegal privileges from the railroads which were bound to ruin every man in the oil business not sharing them with him. Religious emotion and sentiments of charity, propriety and self-denial seem to have taken the place in him of notions of justice and regard for the rights of others.

Unhampered, then, by any ethical consideration, undismayed by the clamor of the Oil Regions, believing firmly as ever that relief for the disorders in the oil business lay in combining and controlling the entire refining interest, this man of vast patience and foresight took up his work. The day after the newspapers of the Oil Regions printed the report of the Congressional Committee on Commerce denouncing the South Improvement Company as "one of the most gigantic and dangerous conspiracies ever attempted," and declaring that if it had not been checked in time it "would have resulted in the absorption and arbitrary control of trade in all the great interests of the

Titusville in 1864   At the time of the discovery of oil in 1859 Titusville was a thrifty country settlement of perhaps 300 inhabitants. It depended chiefly on lumbering for its life. When news of the Drake well reached the outside world, Titusville became the headquarters for an extraordinary inrush of people from all parts of the United States. The rapid growth forced on the town was much more solid than in the case of most towns of the Oil Region. By 1864, as the above picture shows, Titusville was a very good specimen of an American town developed under normal circumstances.

country,"* Mr. Rockefeller and several other members of the South Improvement Company appeared in the Oil Regions. They had come, they explained, to present a new plan of cooperation, and to show the oil men that it was to their interest to go into it. Whether they would be able to obtain by persuasion what they had failed to obtain by assault was now an interesting uncertainty.

*The report of the Committee of Congress which investigated the South Improvement Company was not made until May 7, over a month after the organization was destroyed by the canceling of the contracts with the railroads.

RAY STANNARD BAKER

The Right to Work

The Story of the Non-striking Miners

"The Right to Work" grew out of Ray Stannard Baker's wish to reveal the "other side" of a harrowing 1902 United Mine Workers strike in the anthracite coal fields of Pennsylvania. The "scabs" who continued to work are the focus of Baker's investigative reporting. Approximately 17,000 such miners refused to join the roughly 147,000 anthracite coal miners who walked out in 1902. (See pages 35–36 for some questions raised by Baker's article.)

Public opinion seems to be coming around to the view that the trades' union is here to stay. From many unexpected quarters we hear every now and then a more generous acknowledgment that the organization of labor is not only as inevitable as the combination of capital, but a good thing in itself. At the same time, and from the same fair minds, you hear expressions of passionate indignation at the abuse of power by unions. This means that public opinion is beginning to distinguish between unionism and the sins of unionists, as it is between organized capital and the sins of capitalists.

Clear-headed labor leaders say that violence hurts the union cause, and they denounce it in general. In general, too, violence of the old brick-throwing sort has decreased. It has not disappeared, however, but has taken on a subtler, more deliberate, more terrible form, in many cases, nowadays. Consequently, conditions arise which make liberty and the pursuit of happiness, not to speak of life itself, well nigh impossible to certain of the strikers' fellow men and citizens. The public at large, and often the leaders of unions, do not realize these conditions. But it is manifestly the duty of both to understand them clearly.

We believe that the presentation of the facts—the conditions under which the seventeen thousand non-striking miners worked—will be helpful to the public, which is the final arbiter, and beneficial to those also who have in charge the administration of labor unions. Mr. Baker was, therefore, asked to make an impartial investigation and report, and the following article is the result.   —The Editor

While the right to enter upon a strike is and must be conceded as a right belonging to the personal freedom of working men, this much must ever be demanded, and in the name of the same principal of freedom under which the men act who refuse to work; that they should cease to work must in no

*way interfere with the liberty of others who may wish to work. The personal
freedom of the individual citizen is the most sacred and precious inheritance
of America. The constitution and the laws authorize it. The spirit of the
country proclaims it, the prosperity of the people, the very life of the nation,
require it.*   —Archbishop Ireland

During the closing weeks of the great coal strike, seventeen thousand men
were at work in and around the anthracite coal mines. More than seven
thousand of these were old employees of the companies, long resident in the
communities where they worked, with knowledge of the conditions of life there
existing. Of the remaining ten thousand, part was made up of workers
recruited from one section of the coal fields into another, men who dared not
work in their home villages, but ventured employment at collieries where they
were not personally known; and part consisted of men having no special
knowledge of mining, recruited from neighboring farms or more distant cities.

It seems profoundly important that the public should know exactly who
these seventeen thousand American workers really were, how they fared, and
why they continued to work in spite of so much abuse and even real danger.
This inquiry may be made without bias, without contravening the rights of
labor to organize, or impugning the sincerity of the labor leader, or defending
the operator.

In order, therefore, to learn more of these non-striking workers I visited a
large number of them, their families, and their neighbors, union and non-union,
in various parts of the anthracite regions, reaching them both in their homes
and at their work in and around the mines. I saw the men themselves in each
case, examining at first hand the evidence of their difficulties and dangers,
recording exactly the reasons they gave for continuing to work, securing
corroboration and further light from all sources, both union and non-union.
The account of all the cases investigated would fill an entire number of this
magazine; those here given are typical of the conditions generally prevailing,
and show what the strike signified to the so-called scab, the non-striking
worker.

The first man visited was David Dick, of Old Forge, a small town south of
Scranton. I was led to visit Mr. Dick by a letter bearing his signature published
in the Scranton *Tribune*. Here is the letter:

MR. DICK'S VERSION OF THE ATTEMPT TO KILL HIM

Editor, *Scranton Tribune*
Sir: Your paper this morning (Monday) contained an account of the recent
attempt on my life, which has several inaccuracies. I therefore send you a
correct version, for I think the public ought to know how some persons are

treated in this so-called "free country." On Tuesday evening, September 23, my next-door neighbor, Edward Miller, called at my house and spent some time with us. Shortly after 11 o'clock he left us to go home. I accompanied him to the gate in front of our house. Just as we said "good-night" I turned to reenter the house. Two shots were fired behind me; the shots whistled past my head and lodged in the door in front of me. The night was dark and it was impossible to see any one. My wife is an invalid. Imagine the shock when my family realized that a deliberate attempt had been made on my life.

A short time ago, my son, James Dick, had his home attacked at night by an angry mob. The windows were smashed and the house so damaged that he had to move his family out and come to my place for shelter. Now, why these depredations? Because my son and I try to earn a living for our families. I have been in this country thirty years, and have worked all these years as an engineer. I have tried all my life to live peaceably with all men. I am not a member of the union or any other organization, except the Christian church. When the order was given for engineers to quit work, like many others, I did not obey the orders. Why should I? The company had given me a support in return for my work—I considered myself fairly treated; I had no grievance.

Further, I disagreed with the policy of destruction and revenge which the proposed flooding of the mines implied. I admired the attitude of Mr. Mitchell in the strike two years ago, when he said the property of the companies should be protected, and went so far as to say that men who served as deputies should not be discriminated against when the strike ended. Now, all this is reversed, and I claim my right as a free man to do what my conscience approves.

My forefathers died in Scotland for what they believed to be right, and now, once for all, let me say that I propose to work for my home and loved ones. If I am murdered for this, then I ask my enemies to face me in the daylight and not come skulking around a man's house in the dead of night and fire when my back is turned.

No attempt has been made by the civil authorities to find a clue to the perpetrators of these outrages. I cannot but think if I occupied a position on the other side of the labor question what has happened would be heralded far and wide as an illustration of the tyranny of the operators or their friends. I write in the interest of freedom and justice and the rights of workingmen under the Stars and Stripes in this "land of the free and home of the brave." We have our suspicions of the guilty parties, and if we are correct, they are not far away from us.   David Dick

Old Forge, September 29, 1902

I found Mr. Dick in his engine house at No. 2 Colliery, Old Forge, a prosperous appearing Scotchman who had a singularly clear way of expressing his decided views. He told me he had written the letter, and would reassert all it said. He had come to this country without money, and had been able to save enough to purchase himself a good home of his own. He was a member of the Scotch Presbyterian Church. The company, he said, had always treated him well, and he had no reason for striking. He had been repeatedly threatened, once surrounded by a mob of Italians, once shot at, narrowly escaping death, as his letter shows, and he and his family were ostracised by the strikers of the community. But he said he proposed to work or not to work as he saw fit, and that no threat would deter him. Every day he walked over a mile to his work, going unarmed, though he showed me the riot gun which he had in the engine house to protect him in case the colliery was attacked, as it had been at one time.

REASONS OF AN ENGINEER

I talked with Charles Monie, another Scotch engineer of Moosic, Pa., who had worked for twenty-three years in the place he then occupied. He was a man of high intelligence, an elder in the Presbyterian Church of Avoca. He owned a good home, which I visited, and his children were finding good places in the greater world. I asked him why he had remained with the company. I quote his exact words:

"Unionism is all right when it is kept within bounds. But when it says to any man, 'You can't work until we give you permission,' and when it plans to destroy property, I claim that the individual has a right to quit.

"I have got a home over there without a cent of debt on it. I must have my regular wages to support it.

"I have a right to work when I like, for what I like, and for whom I like.

"I thought about this matter, and as long as my conscience approves my course I don't care who is against me. I don't know your beliefs, but I have faith that the great God will protect me, so I am not afraid."

HOW GORMAN WAS CALLED OUT

Another non-union engineer whom I called on in his engine house was J. R. Gorman, of Exeter Shaft, West Pittston, who had worked for the company twenty-five years. As he said, he was a "free born American citizen, not a made citizen." This is his story:

"At the beginning of the strike Paddy Brann, the president of the local union, came to me and said he was requested to inform me that my presence would be required at St. Alban's Hall that evening to discuss the strike.

William Thomas
"I'd rather be discharged than go back on my friends."

"'I can't go,' I said, 'I'm working.'

"'You understand,' he said, 'that when the strike is over you won't have no work.'

"'Won't I?' I said.

"'No sir; we'll see to that, and you won't be able to buy any goods at the store. We'll boycott you.'

"'Partner,' I said to him, 'look here. Don't you bother your head about me; you've got troubles enough of your own.'

"They hung me in effigy and hooted me in the street. I had to go armed, but they didn't dare lay hands on me. I stand on my rights. I won't have anyone coming to me and telling me when I am to work and when I am to quit working. I don't join a union because I object to having some Dago* I never saw before coming and ordering me to stop work or to go to work again. I can think for myself. I don't need any guardians. What is the object of their union anyway? Why strike, pure and simple, causing all this rioting and trouble. Some labor organizations give their members benefits and insurance, help take care of the sick, and bury the dead. Do the mine workers? Not a bit of it. They pay in their money month after month, the officers draw fat salaries, and by and by they all strike, and begin persecuting and assaulting honest men who want to work."

THE BLINDING OF AN ENGINEER

Another engineer whom I met was Abraham Price, of the Dorrance Colliery, Wilkesbarre. He had been with the company for twenty-two years. English by birth, he came to this country when four years old, and had made a place for himself in the life of the town. He never belonged to a union. He was never personally asked by union men to stop work, and had never been interfered with during the strike except to have strikers call him "scab." He said:

"I thought it was best for my own interest to remain at work. The company has done better for me than any union could. I believe that a man should have a right, no matter what his reasons are, to work when and where he pleases without dictation from any one."

Nearly three weeks after the strike was over, I am informed, on pay day, November 16, 1902, Mr. Price, with other non-union men, was assaulted, and his eyes put out with a blow from a stone.

William Thomas, a fine-looking Welsh engineer whom I met at the Exeter Colliery, had this to say concerning his reasons for staying:

"I thought I should be a coward to turn my back on people who had employed me for twenty-nine years and had always treated me well and paid me promptly. I'd rather be discharged than go back on my friends."

ADVENTURES OF AN ENGLISH MINER

I met Hugh Johnson, a licensed miner of Forest City, who had spent nearly all his life in underground work. He was a good type of the English miner, a man of intelligence, a member of the Masonic fraternity, a communicant in the

---

*A derogatory term for a person of Italian origin.

Presbyterian Church, the owner of two houses which he had bought and paid for from his savings, though he is not a vigorous man physically. I found that Johnson had been a member and officer of the union, indeed a delegate to the convention at Shamokin which declared the strike. He said:

"I believe in unions, and I have long been a member, but I could not agree with the methods of the United Mine Workers. I didn't think we had any cause to strike in the first place. I voted against the strike in the convention, but it was carried by the younger element. All the boys—about a third of all the members—are under age, and the Hungarians and Poles are allowed to vote, and they entirely overwhelmed the conservative element. I did not believe in destroying property by calling out the engineers and pump men, but still I staid out with the strikers until I began to see how the relief fund was distributed. I thought it should be share and share alike. I paid my dues regularly, and my expenses were going on, and I got to the point where I had to have help or else mortgage my home. So I applied to the officers of the local and they said: 'You've got property. Why don't you raise money on it?' And they gave me a good hauling over for presuming to ask for help. The men who got the relief were often those who had been intemperate and improvident before the strike—though there were plenty of genuine cases of poverty—and who had shouted loudest for the strike because they had nothing to lose. I know of some cases in which those relieved took out their relief orders at the store in hams and traded them off for beer. Now that system is putting a premium on improvidence, and fining every man who has saved up any money. As long as they do that of course, the crowd that hasn't anything to lose is going to keep on striking."

A NON-UNION MAN'S DAUGHTER

Mr. Johnson went back to work in the mines, and the union began at once a series of persecutions to compel him to come out. The school board, which was composed of strikers, refused to employ his daughter, who was an experienced teacher, on the ground that she was a "scab." His boy was hooted in school. He himself and other workmen were surrounded one night by a mob which shouted "Kill them! Kill them!" Stones were thrown and several men were injured, but Johnson was fortunately unhurt. Some of the stores refused to sell goods to him or any of his family, but he continued to work, and is working yet. All these things were done by his neighbors and friends, among whom he had lived an honorable life for years.

Many of the men who stayed at work, especially those of the less intelligent class, could, apparently, give no very definite reasons for their act.

J. R. Gorman (at right), who says he was always used well by the Company and sees no reason for going back on his employers

BELLAS, THE "SCAB"

One particularly determined worker was a teamster named Bellas, of the Lehigh Company. They heaped a mock grave in front of his house and set up the inscription:

> **"HERE LIES THE BODY**
> **OF BELLAS THE SCAB."**

That did not bother Bellas, nor did any of the threats. Once when they stopped him he said, "My father fought for this country up in the Wyoming

Valley during the Revolutionary War, and I think I've got a right to work where I please."

At another time they surrounded him and asked him for his union card. He pulled a revolver out of his boot with the remark:

"Here's my card."

They stoned his house, hung him in effigy, and fired at him at night. Part of the time, to prevent his house from being blown up, he watched half the night and his son the other half.

STRUGGLES OF THE SNYDER FAMILY

At Wilkesbarre I met John Snyder, a non-striking worker, and his wife. Snyder is a strong-built young fellow, brought up in the coal regions, a fireman by trade, though he never had worked in the mines until this summer. His wife had been a shopgirl in New York City. Just before the strike began she inherited a legacy of $450.

"When we got that," she said, "we thought that now we could have a little home of our own—I mean we could start one."

But the legacy was small, and homes were costly, so Mrs. Snyder finally went out of the city to Stanton Hill, and bought a lot in a miners' neighborhood, paying $100 for it. Then her husband and his father built a house, mostly of second-hand lumber, leaving the plastering until Snyder should be able to save something from his wages. There was now just money enough left to furnish the house meagerly, and they moved into it, with what joy one may imagine. At last they had a place, a home, in the world. Mrs. Snyder bought a hive of bees, her husband fitted up a chicken-house and made a little garden, hoping thus to add to their income and make the life of their children more comfortable. Every penny they possessed was expended on the home. But Snyder was an industrious fellow, did not "touch, taste, nor handle," as his wife told me, and they knew that he could easily earn enough to support them comfortably.

In the meantime, however, the great strike was on, and every sort of job not connected with the mines was seized upon by union men who were willing to work for almost nothing while the strike lasted, so that Snyder, in order that his family might not be reduced to starvation, was forced, as he told me, to go to work in the mines. He had been thus employed barely four days when one of his neighbors—an Irish striker—came to him. Snyder thus reported to me the conversation which ensued:

"'You're working, are you?'

"'No,' I said.

"'We've got spies on you, and we find that you're firing at the Dorrance.'

"'I am a citizen,' I said, 'and I have a right to work where I please.'

"'Well, I tell you,' he said, 'you can't scab and live here. You ought to be killed, and you'll find your house blown up some morning if you don't quit.'

"Then a big crowd gathered, mostly Irish, and began to yell 'Scab! Kill him! Kill him!' and throw stones at me. I jumped on my bicycle and escaped."

Snyder now remained within the stockade at the Dorrance colliery day and night, fearing death if the strikers caught him, leaving his wife and two babies in the new home on the hill, not dreaming that any harm would come to defenceless women. But crowds, both grown men and boys, gathered daily under the trees near the house, and every time Mrs. Snyder appeared they hooted at her, often insultingly, sometimes threateningly. After a few days of this treatment she became so fearful of personal injury—for she had seen more than one account in the newspapers of what had happened to the wives of non-striking workers—that she took her babies and, having not even money enough to pay car-fare, fled to the city, where she found shelter for the night. For several days she returned to her home to feed the chickens and look after the bees, always subjected coming and going to the jeers and insults of her neighbors. One day she found that her bees had swarmed, and that the swarm was attached to a near-by tree. Here was the first of the increase. She tried her best to get them down and rehived, but, not strong and a woman, she could not do it. Venturing even insult, she ran out to the men on the hill asking help. Not a man of them would assist her. Instead, they hooted her back to her home, and presently she saw her bees rise and disappear to the hills. She could not tell this part of the story without a quivering lip and a tearful eye.

THEIR HOUSE BROKEN INTO

A few days later she returned to find that her home had been entered, her new lamp smashed, a prized clock stolen, her husband's trunk broken open, rifled, and thrown out of the window. In terror she started back toward the city, but turned back to get her canary bird and two or three pet chickens, which, fortunately, she carried away with her. There was nothing now but to desert the new home. The terrified woman sought her husband, but he dared not leave the colliery, though he finally succeeded in getting an advance of $5 on his wages. With this money in hand, Mrs. Snyder hurriedly employed a drayman to move her furniture. When the team reached the house, however, the drivers were stopped by the crowd. She told me they shouted at her: "We'll kill you and your husband if it takes twenty years. Your house will go up in smoke."

And they turned back the teams, not permitting the removal of any of the furniture. In desperation, now, at the prospect of seeing her little home destroyed, Mrs. Snyder went to Mr. Mitchell's headquarters in the Hart Hotel. She told me she had read somewhere that Mr. Mitchell wanted to have no violence committed—that he had promised to prevent violence to non-union men and the blowing up of houses. She met John Fallon, one of Mr. Mitchell's assistants and chairman of the district board of the union, and to him she told her story.

"Why, yes," he said, "I'll see to that; I'll go right out now"—looking at his watch.

THE TRAGEDY OF A HOME

Mrs. Snyder went away relieved. The next morning when she climbed Stanton Hill and looked up to see her home its place was vacant. She found only a cellar full of ashes. The chicken-house was also gone, and of all the chickens not one was left. Even the bees had been burned up, and the little garden was trampled and ruined. An old family dog that had recently brought a family of pups to the house was the only creature left, wandering about whining, looking for her pups. In the telling of this part of their story neither Mr. nor Mrs. Snyder could keep back the tears.

They searched in the ashes, hoping to find something left, but there was not even any remains of their cook stove, or sewing machine, or bed springs, and they learned subsequently—so they told me—that their house had been looted before burning, and that the furniture had been distributed among their neighbors on the hill. Everything was gone. Mrs. Snyder did not even have left a change of clothing for her children. While she and her mother were looking into the ruins the crowd gathered and hooted "Scab, scab! Dynamite them!" so the two helpless women turned back toward the city.

Fresh from her loss, Mrs. Snyder went to see John Fallon, who said:

"I didn't see about it in the newspapers."

Snyder continued to work until the strike was over and the union men came back to the colliery. At once every means was exerted by the strikers to displace non-union workers, Snyder among them, and such influence was brought to bear that the foreman finally discharged Snyder, and when I saw him two weeks after the strike closed he was still out of work, though the company had offered him another position. And Mrs. Snyder has been haunting the second-hand stores of Wilkesbarre, hoping against hope that some of her household goods may be pawned by the thieves, and that she may thus recover them.

I asked Snyder why he did not try to have the criminals arrested.

"In the first place," he said, "if they were arrested they'd never be punished, because everybody is in favor of the strikers, and they could get all their friends to swear they were not present when the house was burned. Besides, I am afraid they'd take it out of me if I did anything."

So nothing has been done, and it seems likely, from what I can learn, that nothing ever will be done to bring the perpetrators of these outrages to justice.

The case of the Snyders is by no means exceptional. There were many instances which I investigated of similar persecution.

THE MURDER OF JAMES WINSTONE

"All we want is investigation," a strike leader said to me. "Now, these murders they talk about. Look into them and you will find that they were the result of the presence of the armed coal and iron police, who were mostly city thugs with orders to shoot and kill. It's a trick of the operators to try to lay all the blame for disturbances on us; they want to work up public sentiment against us." So I went from Scranton to look into the case of James Winstone, of Olyphant.

Olyphant is a more than usually prosperous mining town of some 6,100 inhabitants, nearly all mine workers, over seventy per cent. of whom own their own homes. The population is very diverse, being made up of some dozen different nationalities, but with an unusually large proportion of the English, Welsh, and Irish, the better elements among the miners.*

James Winstone lived in a neighborhood known as Grassy Island, of which he was the foremost citizen, having by far the best home and the most means.

His home was really a pretty place, a two-story house with trees in front, which Winstone himself set out, an arbor where there was shade in summer, a fine garden in which Winstone grew vegetables, and was experimenting with grapes. I came in by the back door to a shining kitchen, spotlessly clean. Indeed, the home was more than comfortably furnished, with an organ, books, pictures, and other evidences of enlightenment and comfort. Mrs. Winstone came in and told us quietly and sadly some of her story. Then we went out again through the spotless kitchen, and crossed to the next house, also the property of James Winstone, and the home of his son-in-law, S. J. Lewis, a worker in the mines. Here, too, was every evidence of comfort and spotless

---

*As an indication of the diversity of nationality, Grassy Slope mine, in which James Winstone worked, had 401 adult employees. Of this number 24 were Americans, 48 English, 60 Welsh, 50 Irish, 5 Scotch, 2 Swede, 152 Polish, 5 German, 41 Hungarian, 5 Italian.

cleanness. The daughter, James Winstone's oldest, had been married only a year. Little by little the story came out, mostly through Mr. D. E. Lewis, a highly intelligent Welshman, the foreman of the mine where Winstone and his son-in-law were employed.

THE RISE OF AN ENGLISH MINER

Winstone had been in America only fourteen years, having come from Yorkshire, England. Reaching Pennsylvania without money, he was able, working as a common miner and supporting a family, to save enough in fourteen years to make him the possessor of two fine homes and everything paid for. Mr. D. E. Lewis told me that Winstone averaged a net earning of $3.50 a day, for which he found it necessary to work only five or six hours. His son-in-law, young Lewis, earned $2.26 a day. Winstone was in the prime of life, forty-eight years old, with a wife and three children. His wife told me with sad pride how he had been respected in his community. He was treasurer, she said, for eight years of the Lackawanna Accident Fund, a member of the Sons of St. George and of the Red Men, and even, at one time, an officer in the United Mine Workers. She said he had not an enemy in the world, that all he wanted was to live peaceably and see his sons properly educated. He meant to keep them in school until they could work into good positions. They had done well in the mines, but they hoped the boys would do something better.

Winstone, a natural leader, opposed the strike from the beginning, as did others of the conservative element. He asserted publicly that he saw no cause for striking, that any man who was willing to work and was temperate could get ahead, that there was too much agitation. But he and the conservatives were overwhelmed and the strike declared. Winstone went out with the others, found employment for several weeks outside the mines at a fraction of his former wages, and then came back home. He now saw that he must mortgage his property to live. He went to the union, and was told that he would be given no assistance. He had property and he could raise money on that. This, however, he refused to do.

So Winstone went back to the mine to work. His son-in-law, S. J. Lewis, had already gone back, in company with some of the other mine workers of the community. Immediately the strikers began their tactics of intimidation and threats. Every morning and evening they gathered in the road and hooted Winstone, Lewis, Doyle, and others on their way to work. Sometimes they gathered in front of his home, threateningly, but Winstone would not be

cowed. One night a larger crowd than usual appeared, and Patrick Fitzsim-
mons, secretary of the local and auditor of the general assembly, stood up and
shouted a violent tirade against scabs. One of the things he said, reported to
me by Mr. Lewis, was: "If there were half a dozen of loyal union men like me
there wouldn't be one of the scabs that would dare to go to work."

These crowds were composed of Irish and English, with a large rallying
force of Poles and others. Most of them were Winstone's neighbors and
fellow-workmen, and many of them had been his good friends.

A week before the final tragedy, a committee waited on Winstone and
requested him to stop work, threatening him if he did not. Winstone told them
that he would not desert his place.

The persecutions now became so severe that Winstone and Lewis, instead
of going to the mine by the road, were accustomed to go back through the
garden, climb a fence, cross the rear of a lot occupied by a Polish miner named
Harry Shubah, a neighbor well known to Winstone, and join William Doyle,
another non-union man, the three men going together. They carried no
arms.

DAY OF THE TRAGEDY

The morning of September 25th was rainy. Winstone and Lewis had gone
down through the garden. When they had climbed the fence into Shubah's
yard, Lewis took his father-in-law's arm, and was holding an umbrella over
his head. Suddenly, hearing a noise, he glanced behind and saw Harry
Simuralt, another Polish neighbor with whom both were well acquainted.
Simuralt had a club lifted. Lewis cried:

"Don't strike us with that."

The words were hardly out of his mouth when he was felled to the earth.
Jumping up again, half dazed, he ran toward Doyle's house. Hearing Winstone
shout, "Don't kill me," he glanced behind and saw several men pounding him
with clubs. Lewis himself was now pursued and struck in the back with a
heavy stick, but he succeeded in escaping. The assaulters having pounded
Winstone to their satisfaction, left him lying in his blood. He was carried into
Doyle's house, where he died a few hours later without regaining consciousness. Lewis was in bed three weeks.

Everything evidently had been plotted beforehand. The murderers were
perfectly sober, making an evidently planned escape by train. Fortunately
they were arrested at Hoboken, New Jersey, and brought back to Scranton,
where they are now in jail. According to Lewis, the three men most concerned

James Winstone and His Family
Winstone was killed in the yard of a neighbor on his way to work,
September 25, 1902.

were Harry Simuralt, Harry Shubah, and Tom Priston, all Polish miners, union
men, and strikers—all near neighbors of Winstone, long known to him. The
astonishing thing is that they had been in the country for years and spoke
English well; one of them, Simuralt, owned his own home, a very comfortable
place. Foreman Lewis told me that they all bore good reputations as industrious and temperate workers.

It is interesting, as showing the difficulty of protecting life, that seven
hundred soldiers were camped within less than half a mile of the scene of this
murder.

A MURDER IN THE FOG

Through some peculiarity of location, the valley of the Susquehanna is singularly subject to fogs—not unlike those of southern England, appearing before dawn and often continuing until long after sunrise. Such a fog filled the valley on the early morning of September 8, 1902. It was so thick that a man could see only a few paces before him—familiar houses, fences, road-marks, seemed mysterious. It was on this foggy morning that a number of important things were happening in the vicinity of the Maltby Colliery. Though no one could see any evidence of life, nor hear any sound, yet men were gathering from several directions—men who hated one another. There were three parties of them, all armed. On the previous Saturday night there had been a joint meeting of three locals of the United Mine Workers of America—the Luzerne, the Broderick, and the Maltby. It was a special occasion. Reports were made by an officer that the company intended to add a large number of non-union men to its force at the Maltby Colliery on the following Monday morning. This news was received with jeers, and after much discussion a motion was made and passed calling upon all the members of the three locals to be present at the entrance to the colliery on Monday morning. Great secrecy was enjoined, but there was a man present whose business it was to listen to just such news; he carried the word immediately to the officials of the Lehigh Valley Coal Company. Sheriff Jacobs being notified, armed deputies were provided to escort the non-union men on Monday morning. This accounted for two of the parties gathered in the fog. The mob appeared in great force, many armed with clubs, some having large iron nuts at the end; some with stones; others with cheap revolvers. Lining themselves up along the roadways, they awaited the coming of the car with the non-union men.

In the meantime another party of two men was out in the fog. Sistieno Castelli and his friend and brother-in-law, Kiblotti, were going hunting. Castelli was a peaceable citizen, whose family was hungry. He had his gun on his shoulder, and was tramping up the Lackawanna Railroad tracks on his way to the hills, hoping to find some rabbits or squirrels. Just as he and his friend reached a point behind the house of John Keeler, outside foreman of the mine, the car with the non-union men had come to a stop. The mob, fully expecting to surprise the non-union men and have them instantly at their mercy, came up out of the fog to find themselves facing armed deputies. Under cover of this surprise the non-union men were hurried into Keeler's house, guarded by the deputies. The mob, gathering quickly, foresaw that an attempt would be made to rush the workmen from Keeler's house by the back way to the mine, so they turned and streamed up the tracks of the Lackawanna

Railroad, between the colliery and the foreman's home. And here they came suddenly upon Castelli and Kiblotti there in the fog. Castelli cried out. Some one, said to be a Hungarian, struck him a frightful blow on the head, felling him to the earth. And then they seized his shotgun, placed the muzzle against Castelli's body, and pulled the trigger. In the meantime several others pitched upon his companion, but in the confusion Kiblotti succeeded in escaping. The mob then turned their attention to Castelli, in their fury horribly beating his lifeless body. Having glutted their passion, they turned the body over and went through the pockets, and this is what they found—a union card and a receipt for dues paid, showing that Castelli was a good union man, a member of the Broderick Local No. 452. They had killed him and left another widow and children, visiting upon him the fate they had planned for the non-union men. In the meantime the deputies and their charges were safe in the colliery.

A WIFE'S EXPERIENCE

In the list read before the Arbitration Commission of the men murdered during the strike was the name of John Colson, and the memorandum, "Non-union man beaten to death at Shenandoah." I went to Shenandoah to learn more of the story of John Colson.

At first I could find no record of any workman named Colson. Shenandoah had her share of riot and bloodshed, but Colson was not remembered among those injured. But I finally heard of a man of that name who had been working at Shamokin, and I went down to find John Colson, not dead, but living and working tenaciously after an experience that would have daunted most men. He is an English born engineer. Previous to the strike he had lived at Gilberton, working as an engineer, the best position at the colliery. He did not believe in the strike, nor in the order withdrawing the engineers, and he had not been slow in saying so. But he went out with the other strikers and remained a month; then he went to work at the Henry Clay Colliery, at Shamokin. Spies at once found him out, but, living in a car close to the colliery, they could not reach him personally, so they brought to bear the usual pressure on his wife and family at Gilberton. She was boycotted at some of the stores, so that she could not buy the necessaries of life. She was jeered and insulted in the streets, and her home was stoned.

"Every night," she told me, "I was afraid to go to bed for fear they would blow up my home with dynamite. They did dynamite three houses in the same neighborhood."

HOW COLSON WAS ATTACKED

So she finally wrote to her husband that she could bear it no longer, and he rented a house in Shamokin, and told her to move the furniture. This she tried to do, but the teamsters refused to assist her, and she feared that if she attempted to get away the strikers would attack her. Accordingly, Colson bought furniture at Shamokin to fit up a new home. On the evening of October 7 he came up from his work with several coal and iron police to look after the arrangement of his purchases, and when he had finished he started back alone along the railroad tracks. The police had warned him of his danger, and he had, indeed, already been stoned, and yet, naturally fearless, he was going back alone. Having a revolver, he thought he could defend himself. A trainload of soft coal was passing; a mob of men appeared, shouting at him threateningly. He reached to draw his revolver, and a man on one of the cars dropped a huge block of coal on his head. Colson fell in his tracks, and after further beating him, the mob robbed him of his revolver and a new pair of boots, and left him for dead. For three days he lay unconscious in the hospital, and there, slowly, with careful nursing, he recovered, and as soon as he could walk went back to work again. His wife now succeeded in getting an undertaker from an adjoining town to move her goods, under guard of a deputy, and they settled at Shamokin. I found them in a comfortable, pleasant home—two boys at work in the mines and a comely daughter.

THE MOTHER OF A NON-UNION MAN

In this case of John Colson I had an opportunity of seeing what it means, socially, for a man to work during a strike. At Mahoney City, in the last house in the town, one of the dingy red company houses, almost in the shadow of an enormous pile of culm, I found John Colson's father and mother. The old miner had just come in from his work, his face and clothing black with coal dust. His wife had hot water ready for him, and a tub stood waiting on her kitchen floor, so that he might wash off the marks of the mine. Yet some of the marks he could not wash off—the blue tatooing of powder which covered his face with ugly scars. Five years before he had been in a mine explosion. A careless Hungarian, cross-cutting through the coal, had set off his blast without giving warning, and Colson had been taken from the mine for dead, but he finally lived, blue-scarred, wholly blind in one eye and almost blind in the other. He was an old man even then; he had been mining, here and in England, for nearly fifty years, and his seven sons, miners all, told him that he might rest the

Typical Miners' Homes at Forest City

remainder of his days. So for four years previous to the great strike he had lived quietly a comfortable old age, he and his wife alone in the red house at the end of the village, their sons and daughters around them.

But with the strike came hard times, and the sons, though willing to help their parents, had many mouths of their own to feed, and by the time the miners were ordered back to work in October they were all in straightened circumstances, so that old John Colson was compelled to go back into the mines. He told me he was doing a boy's job now—turning a fan in a deep working, and that he earned only 75 cents a day, but he was glad to be employed again. The mother told me with pride of her boys—Anthony with his family of eight children, her other boys, and the married daughters. And so we came to speak of John, her oldest son, the one reported beaten to death. She flushed at the mention of his name, said at first that she would have nothing to say about him, and then, bitterly:

"He might better be dead, for he's brought disgrace on the name."

All the brothers, the old miner said, had been members of the union, and had come out when the strike was called, but John had gone back to work.

"He deserved all he got," said his mother. "He wasn't raised a scab."

THE HARDEST PENALTY OF ALL

Then she told how, when he lay hovering between life and death in the hospital, she had not gone to him once, and yet she wanted so much to know whether he would live or die that she called up the hospital on the telephone.

"But I didn't give my name," she said, "so he didn't know about it."

Since he was well again none of the family had visited him or paid the least attention to him. The strike had wholly crushed all family feeling. John was not again to be recognized.

Such a story as this gives a faint idea of the meaning of a strike in the coal fields.

NONE OF THESE INCIDENTS EXCEPTIONAL

I could, as I have said, fill a whole number of this magazine with other narratives of like incidents that I have myself investigated. Those that I have set down here are not chosen as especially flagrant cases; they constitute only a few among scores, even hundreds, of similar tragedies of the great coal strike.

Concerning Three Articles in this Number of McClure's, and a Coincidence that May Set Us Thinking

How many of those who have read through this number of the magazine noticed that it contains three articles on one subject? We did not plan it so; it is a coincidence that the January *McClure's* is such an arraignment of American character as should make every one of us stop and think. How many noticed that?

The leading article, "The Shame of Minneapolis," might have been called "The American Contempt of Law." That title could well have served for the current chapter of Miss Tarbell's History of Standard Oil. And it would have fitted perfectly Mr. Baker's "The Right to Work." All together, these articles come pretty near showing how universal is this dangerous trait of ours. Miss Tarbell has our capitalists conspiring among themselves, deliberately, shrewdly, upon legal advice, to break the law so far as it restrained them, and to misuse it to restrain others who were in their way. Mr. Baker shows labor the ancient enemy of capital, and the chief complainant of the trusts' unlawful acts, itself committing and excusing crimes. And in "The Shame of Minneapolis" we see the administration of a city employing criminals to commit crimes for the profit of the elected officials, while the citizens—Americans of good stock and more than average culture, and honest, healthy Scandinavians—stood by complacent and not alarmed.

Capitalists, workingmen, politicians, citizens—all breaking the law, or letting it be broken. Who is left to uphold it? The lawyers? Some of the best lawyers in this country are hired, not to go into court to defend cases, but to advise corporations and business firms how they can get around the law without too great a risk of punishment. The judges? Too many of them so respect the laws that for some "error" or quibble they restore to office and liberty men convicted on evidence overwhelmingly convincing to common sense. The churches? We know of one, an ancient and wealthy establishment, which had to be compelled by a Tammany hold-over health officer to put its tenements in sanitary condition. The colleges? They do not understand.

There is no one left; none but all of us. Capital is learning (with indignation at labor's unlawful acts) that its rival's contempt of law is a menace to property. Labor has shrieked the belief that the illegal power of capital is a menace to the worker. These two are drawing together. Last November when a strike was threatened by the yard-men on all the railroads centering in Chicago, the men got together and settled by raising wages, and raising freight rates too. They made the public pay. We all are doing our worst and making the public pay. The public is the people. We forget that we all are the people; that while each of us in his group can shove off on the rest the bill of to-day, the debt is only postponed; the rest are passing it on back to us. We have to pay in the end, every one of us. And in the end the sum total of the debt will be our liberty.

EDITOR'S NOTE: This editorial was written by S. S. McClure to accompany the articles by Steffens, Tarbell, and Baker.

Muckraking and Its Aftermath

A reading of the muckraking essays of Steffens, Tarbell, and Baker provides a starting print for an assessment of their legacy. But this is a very difficult task because the impact of muckraking on early-twentieth-century American politics and society remains something of a historical mystery. Virtually every history of the Progressive period mentions the literature of exposure. But sharp disagreement exists over the significance of muckraking. Historical judgment has tended to divide along two lines. Some commentators stake a large claim, perhaps too large, for muckraking in shaping the reform politics of the early twentieth century. These historians view the muckrakers as influential agents of social change. At the risk of simplifying, this model credits the muckrakers with awakening a sleeping public to the evils of monopoly and the price being paid for political lawlessness. Having seen what had previously been unseen, an aroused citizenry demanded reform. Attentive legislatures responded to the public outcry and the result was an array of reform measures that helped clean up politics, curb political corruption, regulate corporate activity, and improve food, drugs, and meat. While few historians would assert a simple cause-and-effect relationship between muck-raking and reform, many place the two in proximity, leaving vague the question of how specifically one influenced the other.[1]

The temptation to yield to this view of muckraking is very great. It elides ideas and politics, leaving the heroism of the writers apparent, the victory for the public unambiguous, and, perhaps most important, the triumph of democracy complete. At first glance, the facts of early-twentieth-century political history seem to correlate with this optimistic view of muckraking. Ida Tarbell wrote a devastating history of the Standard Oil Company that was published between 1902 and 1904. Two years after it ran, Theodore Roosevelt's administration brought an antitrust suit against Standard Oil, charging the company with restraint of trade. In 1905 Ray Stannard Baker wrote a series of essays on the railroads for *McClure's* that influenced President Roosevelt's efforts to set federal guidelines for railroad rates. A year later, at Roosevelt's behest, Congress passed legislation that expanded government regulation of the railroads in the Hepburn Act. Lincoln Steffens alerted Americans to a national pattern of influence dealing by business interests in state and local politics. A year after publication of *The Shame of the Cities* (1904), state after state passed election reform laws, regulations on lobbying, and restrictions on corporate campaign contributions. Finally, and most infamously, in 1906 Upton Sinclair published *The Jungle,* his gruesome account of conditions in the meatpacking plants of Chicago, hoping to inspire sympathy for the workers and win converts to socialism. "I aimed at the public's heart," he later lamented, "and by accident I hit it in the stomach." Four months later Congress passed the Meat Inspection Act of 1906 regulating meat production and processing.[2]

It seems reasonable to assume that something more than coincidence was at work in the timing of the muckrakers' exposés and the notable legislative reform activity of the early twentieth century. But it is equally prudent to suspect that additional factors were at work in turning the criticism of muckrakers into legislative victories. As noted earlier, Standard Oil had been the subject of critical scrutiny well before 1902; indeed, Tarbell drew on previous exposés to construct her own history. In addition, legal efforts to curb Standard Oil had been pursued at the state level well before Ida Tarbell wrote her history. The United States Industrial Commission paid particular attention to the company in its 1901 report. Tarbell had relied on the commission's research to determine details of Standard's railroad rebates. Legislative means of combating monopoly had been the subject of political debate—and, indeed, congressional action—well before the onset of muckraking. By the time Tarbell began her series, the Roosevelt administration was moving toward a flurry of antitrust activity.

Election reform too had been an important dimension of late-nineteenth-century politics. The early years of the twentieth century brought significant new developments, but the trend owed something to reform pressures that predated the arrival of the muckrakers. It is important to remember, too, that Steffens took his lead from *local* disclosures of political corruption. That fact complicates any interpretation that would credit Steffens with discovering the role of business interests in shaping urban politics. Finally, Baker began his essays on the railroads *after* Roosevelt had laid down the gauntlet on railroad regulation in a 1904 address to Congress that proposed expanding the power of the Interstate Commerce Commission to set railroad rates. These are just a few of the historical realities that complicate our understanding of muckraking. They suggest that the literature of exposure needs to be understood as a product of the social and political environment at least as much as an independent force that shaped the reform climate of the early twentieth century.[3]

Certainly that conclusion would echo the views of historians who have placed relatively little stock in the concrete political consequences of muckraking. The Achilles heel of the muckrakers, according to these historians, was apparent in three areas, each of which weakened the impact of their exposés. The first weakness lay in the muckrakers' apparent lack of a sophisticated analysis of the American polity and economy. Again to simplify, scholars critical of the muckrakers stress their naive tendency to focus on individual cases of wrongdoing at the expense of developing the institutional matrix within which political corruption and monopoly occurred. In effect, these historians turn against the muckrakers what they and perhaps their audiences found to be one of their great strengths—the ability to personalize and humanize broad social, economic, and political problems in highly specific and concrete ways.[4]

But were the muckrakers' efforts to particularize wrongdoing incompatible with a structural understanding of   industrial society? Certainly Steffens believed that more than individual malfeasance produced the "shameful" state of urban politics. His essays suggested that business had played a major role in the corruption of politics and that the election of "honest" officeholders would do nothing to address this fundamental problem in American government. Ray Stannard Baker understood the importance of trade unions to the progress of America's working class. But he was also alert to the perils of corruption in the union leadership that might undermine the hopes of laboring women and men.

A second criticism historians have leveled against the muckrakers is their failure to advance solutions to the problems they exposed. Implicit in this complaint is the somewhat paradoxical notion that the journalists had an obligation to do more than simply publicize and investigate. We might well reflect on why we would expect an activist role from these early-twentieth-century reporters that today might well be seen as a compromise of objectivity.[5]

Finally, the muckrakers' appeals to a collective public conscience as a means of effecting change have been dismissed as unsophisticated by some historians. It is worth asking whether modern political conditions have shaped this somewhat cynical sense of the American polity. Steffens, Tarbell, and Baker were hardly innocents, if we judge by their hard-hitting, and even courageous, efforts to publicize the evils of industrial society. How do we square their willingness to expose these terrible problems with a presumed naiveté in their judgments of the capacities of American society? Perhaps for this generation there was no necessary contradiction between their realistic sense of the daunting problems of their time and a faith in the ability of Americans to change the course of history.

Charged with providing a superficial analysis, no solutions, and ineffectual reform ideals, the muckrakers emerge, in the biting critique of one historian, as "journalists rather than thinkers, with commonplace talents and middle-class values, incapable of serious or radical critiques. A few, at least, were opportunists." At the same time, it should be stressed that historians have also drawn a distinction between good muckraking and bad, basing their judgments of the former on the fact-based, careful, and "responsible" work of writers such as Steffens, Baker, and Tarbell and the latter on the overblown, exaggerated, and sensationalist essays of writers such as Thomas Lawson, author of a series on financial speculation entitled "Frenzied Finance." The coexistence of both styles has been seen as a factor that further weakened the power of muckraking.[6]

THE CONTEMPORARY RESPONSE TO MUCKRAKING

How, then, can we make sense of these diverging visions of the muckrakers' legacy? Perhaps the best way is to again use the analytical tools of history. One of the most interesting elements of the historical debate over the muck-rakers is how *closely it mirrors the response to the muckrakers that emerged in their own time.* Virtually all of the criticisms that historians have leveled against the muckrakers, and much of the praise too, was voiced by Tarbell's, Baker's, and Steffens's contemporaries. Perhaps this reflects, in part, modern historians' reliance on early characterizations of the muckrakers for evidence. But it may also reflect persistent conflicts regarding the role of social criticism in the transformation of American society.

Certainly the muckrakers had their numerous boosters in the early twentieth century. *The Arena* claimed in 1906, for example,

that there is not in the United States today another band of high-minded, intelligent and conscientious workers who have greater faith in the power of moral ideals, greater faith in the future of free government, greater love for that which is noble, just and true, greater devotion to the Republic, or more moral heroism than the men and women who in the great magazines have so fearlessly, toilsomely, ably and effectively battled to expose rotten conditions in modern high finance, the trusts, the corporations, and in public. America owes a last debt of gratitude to such patriotic writers.[7]

Countless magazine essays, newspaper articles, and book reviews credited the muckrakers with such heroism. *The New York Times* praised Tarbell's work as a model of objectivity, and another journal proclaimed that *"History of Standard Oil* is to the present time the most remarkable book of its kind ever written in this country." Like some modern historians, many contemporaries were convinced that the muckrakers were a critical force in advancing political reform and a more just society. They described the reporters' essays as revelations, and they followed with high expectation the public outcry that followed the investigations of the magazines.[8]

Yet other contemporaries harshly criticized the work and intentions of the muckrakers. In a devastating review of *The History of the Standard Oil Company, The Nation* accused Tarbell of writing "for the purpose of intensifying the popular hatred" of the company, a revealing comment affirming that hostility to the trust predated the muckraker. Dismissing the work as "a railing accusation" that would "not be accepted as history," the reviewer poorly predicted the fate of Tarbell's book.[9] Ninety years later, her work was still being praised for its accuracy. In his Pulitzer Prize–winning study of oil, *The Prize,* Daniel Yergin characterized *The History of the Standard Oil Company* as "a work of great clarity and force" and "arguably . . . the single most influential book on business ever published in the United States."[10]

Reviewers in the early twentieth century who disagreed made their case against the muckrakers in terms remarkably predictive of historical judgments that ran against the muckrakers later in the twentieth century. The reporters were charged with being sensationalist in their claims, unsophisticated in their analyses, and ineffectual in their reform ideals. Critic George Alger advanced these charges in the August 1905 *Atlantic Monthly:*

> In the past decade there has grown up in this country a school of incomplete idealists, social reformers, who, in their methods and theories, seem to have gone back to the old-time theology. They seek to apply to society as a whole the methods which failed with the individual. From one branch of this cult has come the modern literature of "exposure." They show us our social sore spots, like the three cheerful friends of Job.

Lambasting the muckrakers for their relentless and reckless assaults on financiers and legislators, Alger noted that "few of the writers who so cleverly

point out to us our social sores seem to have any kind of salve in their hands."
He anticipated historians who would later upbraid the muckrakers for provid-
ing simple analyses and individual case studies. "The literature of exposure,"
Alger argued,

> is not criticism in any such sense. For it exposes not the opportunities which
> create temptations, but the individuals who succumb. It seems to arraign,
> not the defects in the social system, but humanity itself. . . . It takes the whole
> burden of moral responsibility from the shoulders of society, and throws it
> all on the individual.[11]

Even sympathetic journals such as *The Independent* believed that the social
criticism of the muckrakers was a political flash in the pan. "The public
conscience has been awakened and wrong-doers have been stricken with
wholesome fear," a 1906 editorial ran. "But henceforth the work of exposing
evil must be transformed into a steady-going, constructive effort to prevent
it."[12]

Yet, as is true of modern treatments of the muckrakers, early-twentieth-
century observers didn't deny muckrakers their place in history. Whether the
opinions were good or ill, there was little question that the exposés of Steffens,
Tarbell, Baker, and the other investigative journalists had hit a public nerve.
During the heyday of muckraking, the magazines that led in promoting the
literature of exposure had a combined readership that has been estimated at
3 million on the conservative side and at 20 million most generously. This in
a nation whose entire population stood at fewer than 80 million in 1900. The
circulation of *McClure's* had actually experienced its greatest period of growth
during the 1890s. From a circulation of less than 30,000 during its inaugural
year, *McClure's* had jumped to 370,000 by 1900. The muckraking years
boosted circulation another 130,000, with advertising that yielded nearly $1
million of revenue in 1906. Clearly muckraking attracted plenty of attention
in the form of an expanded readership. Ironically, it also proved to be a
profitable business venture.[13]

As we think about the public response to muckraking, it is worth attending
to the perceptions of the investigative journalists themselves. Almost immediately after the publication of the January 1903 issue of *McClure's,* Tarbell,
Baker, and Steffens felt acutely aware of their growing celebrity. Ida Tarbell
had already won national recognition for her studies of Napoleon and Lincoln.
But the Standard Oil series in *McClure's* and the book on the same subject that
followed in 1904 enlarged both the circle of her critics and her admiring
following. Traveling in Kansas and Oklahoma in 1905 to cover exploitation
of new oil reserves, Tarbell discovered that she was a celebrity. "It was not
long," she recalled, "before I found I was being taken for something more
serious than a mere journalist."

Conservative Standard Oil sympathizers regarded me as a spy and not infrequently denounced me as an enemy to society. Independent oilmen and radical editors, who were in the majority, called me a prophet. It brought fantastic situations where I was utterly unfit to play the part. . . . Here I was—fifty, fagged, wanting to be let alone while I collected trustworthy information for my articles—dragged to the front as an apostle.

Tarbell resisted the role of "apostle" but she did provide information on the Standard Oil in 1906 to James Garfield, head of the Bureau of Corporations, who was preparing a report on the petroleum industry. The report, which affirmed many of Tarbell's findings regarding rate discrimination, helped lay the groundwork for the federal government's impending antitrust suit. Tarbell herself never claimed any credit for the government's antitrust action. She was too good a historian to play such a reductionist game.[14]

Baker and Steffens were far less reluctant than Tarbell to rise to their fame. "The public response to these articles," Baker said of the January 1903 issue of *McClure's,* "was astonishing. I doubt whether any other magazine published in America ever achieved such sudden and overwhelming recognition. . . . Everybody seemed to be reading them." Baker recalled years later "hundreds of editorials and quotations in the newspapers, a deluge of letters, commendations or attacks in political speeches, even references in sermons." Baker's article "The Right to Work" won him an invitation to lunch with President Roosevelt. The reporter prepared extensive notes on the anthracite strike and an environmental project he had followed in Arizona. The lunch flew by in a blur, and Baker recalled:

As the time drew near for leaving, I began to wonder when the President would ask me for the information upon which I had spent so much time and hard work. I had my heavy brief case in hand when I went up to say good-bye—and my grand plans for enlightening the Government of the United States vanished in a handshake.[15]

Still, the essay led Baker to a closer association with Roosevelt. The two men exchanged several letters in 1905 debating various reform issues. The extent of the reporter's influence on the president is difficult to measure. Baker became increasingly radical in his politics after 1905; he was deeply disappointed with Roosevelt. For Roosevelt the feeling was entirely mutual.[16]

Steffens got an immediate taste of his fame when a lawyer sued *McClure's* for libel (unsuccessfully) after Steffens referred to him as a politician in "The Shame of Minneapolis." Like Tarbell and Baker, Steffens followed up his initial series for *McClure's* with further investigations of corruption in the states. Together with *The Shame of the Cities,* these essays enhanced Steffens's fame. When election time rolled around in 1905, some of the corrupt politicians that Steffens had exposed were booted out of office, and some of the heroes that he had publicized took their place. Many Americans, including Columbia Law professor and future Supreme Court Justice Harlan Fiske Stone, credited Steffens with speeding the pace of political change. "I think you more than any other man," Stone wrote to the muckraker after election day, "may take credit for the result of the elections wherever 'boss or no boss rule' was the issue." Like Baker, Steffens remained in close touch with Theodore Roosevelt. But while outwardly friendly, Roosevelt was not happy with Steffens's new stature as an authority on what was good and what was bad, who was in and who ought to be out in American politics.[17]

We cannot measure the precise impact of Steffens's, Tarbell's, and Baker's writings on the many political reforms that coincided with their essays in *McClure's Magazine*. We do know that their writings were widely read by Americans and heatedly debated by public opinion makers. And in that debate may lie a key to the puzzle of muckraking. Some social scientists who have studied political communications stress that readers tend "to choose periodicals and programs that reinforce pre-existing views." Others note that a small circle of well-informed readers who follow the media can shape public opinion powerfully as they share their views with other, less-informed members of their communities. Furthermore, even if the public reads the press selectively, there is evidence that political leaders use the press to take the measure of prevailing public opinion.

If we apply these findings to the muckrakers, we might hazard a guess that politicians and citizens who followed the literature of exposure may well have played a central role in adding political clout to muckraking. It has been estimated that politicians at the turn of the century thought in terms of a "voting public" of roughly 13 to 15 million citizens. It has further been estimated (at the low end) that the circulation of the muckraking magazines was approximately 3 million. Women, who could not vote, were probably frequent readers of magazines. Other nonvoters, such as aliens, must have also been represented among the readership. We can't assume, in other words, that all the readers of the muckraking magazines belonged to the electorate. Or, indeed, that all readers would have voted to oust the bosses and curb the special interests. Nonetheless voters and nonvoters who followed the work of muckrakers may already have been sympathetic to the political slant of the investigative journalists. The facts amassed by the muckrakers could certainly have powerfully affirmed their biases and added weight to their opinions. It may be that by probing further into the "structure of public opinion" and into politicians' *perceptions* of public opinion, historians can better specify how the muckrakers' work entered the arena of politics.[18]

A journalist writing in 1910 for *Twentieth Century Magazine* pursued this approach in an effort to demonstrate the powerful impact of muckraking.

William Kittle noted the wide discrepancy in readership between conservative and muckraking magazines. He offered a fascinating (if self-serving) analysis of the articles and editorials published in eleven major magazines between 1904 and 1906, including the intrepid *Twentieth Century*. Only ninety articles defended "some special privilege," "property rights," and "monopoly"; three hundred articles "defended the larger interests of society," by which he meant liberal reform ideals. ("In one or two cases," he noted, "was the article so scholarly that the reader could not tell what the writer was driving at.") Presumably drawing on circulation figures, Kittle estimated that the ninety essays supporting monopoly rights were read by roughly four million Americans. The three hundred articles supporting "economic and social betterment" had an audience of six million, he asserted. But, he added, "these 6,000,000 gave to the larger American public, from the platform and in the press, the doctrine of economic rights and the inherent injustices of certain monopolies and special privileges." Here, years before the studies of experts in political communication, was an attempt to chart the transmission of muckraking from the realm of ideas to politics through public opinion analysis.[19]

Political commentator Walter Lippmann also stressed the power of public opinion as a critical factor in muckraking. A trenchant analysis of the literature of exposure in his *Drift and Mastery* (1914) argued that "it is not very illuminating to say that this smear of suspicion has been worked up by the muckrakers."

> If business and politics really served American need, you could never induce people to believe so many accusations against them. It is said, also, that the muckrakers play for circulation, as if that proved their insincerity. But the mere fact that muckraking was what people wanted to hear is in many ways the most important revelation of the whole campaign. There is no other way of explaining the quick approval which the muckrakers won. They weren't voices crying in a wilderness or lonely prophets who were stoned. They demanded a hearing; it was granted. They asked for belief; they were believed. . . . There must have been real causes for dissatisfaction, or the land notorious for its worship of success would not have turned so savagely upon those who had achieved it.

Lippmann stressed that as American visions "of what a democratic state might do" enlarged in the early twentieth century, so did fear of corruption. Industrial society had created new expectations for government that heightened the public's sensitivity to the business corruption of politics. "When men's vision of government enlarged," Lippmann argued, "the cost of corruption and inefficiency rose: for they meant the blighting of the whole possibility of the state." According to Lippmann, the muckrakers—for all their faults, and he found many—played an important role in applying to business and politics an emerging public standard of ethics in government. "The literature of exposure arose," he drolly observed, "because the world has been altered radically, not because Americans fell in love with honesty."[20]

THE DEMISE OF MUCKRAKING

A final puzzle remains for students of muckraking. That is to consider what happened to the literature of exposure that achieved such enormous recognition in the early twentieth century. While historians differ in the dates of their death notices for muckraking, many agree that the movement peaked around 1906. Gradually the magazines devoted less and less space to the articles of investigative journalists. Some magazines folded. Others lost their best muckraking journalists, though not necessarily their penchant for investigative journalism. This was the case with *McClure's*, which experienced the simultaneous defection of Ida Tarbell, Lincoln Steffens, and Ray Stannard Baker when they left with John Phillips in 1906 to join the *American Magazine*.

Finally pushed over the edge by the erratic behavior of S. S. McClure and fed up with his increasingly wild schemes, the three writers pursued new political and literary interests in their essays for the *American Magazine*. This journal, Tarbell noted, "had little genuine muckraking spirit," and, in fact, the founders sought to emphasize "hopeful" things. Tarbell radically reversed what many critics unfairly considered her "antibusiness" creed. She eventually wrote several celebratory accounts of leading American industrialists. Steffens stayed only briefly at the *American Magazine*. He had been radicalized by his years as a muckraker, and drifted toward socialism. By 1908, Steffens too had abandoned muckraking, the literary form that had given life to his best work. He later wound up writing an essay for *McClure's* entitled "The Fame of the Cities." Baker continued to write essays that resembled his earlier work. He turned his attention to race relations while at the *American Magazine*.

Baker also published several works of fiction under the pseudonym of David Grayson, a wandering farmer who reported "Adventures in Contentment" that were full of allegories. Indeed, Baker depicted Grayson at the end of one novel standing high "on the hill Clear" with an unobstructed view of "the gates of the celestial city." It was no coincidence that that was the celestial place Roosevelt had accused the muckrakers of failing to see. S. S. McClure too relinquished his investment in muckraking. In 1911, dire economic circumstances wrested from McClure's hands the magazine that bore his name, though the journal continued to publish under various editors until 1929. But it too was largely out of the muckraking business by 1912.[21]

Historians have advanced various explanations for the decline of muckraking. Some have argued that the literature died from a lack of public interest that inevitably resulted from the muckrakers' relentless literary assault on the magazines. The public simply reached its saturation point, according to these scholars, and moved on in its fickle tastes to more pleasant stories. Other historians reject the theory of death by natural causes and insist on murder by decree. The magazines depended heavily on advertising for revenue and yielded to the efforts of business owners to muzzle muckraking. There is little evidence to support either of these explanations. While it is true that public tastes change, it seems ahistorical to ignore the rather abrupt fall-off in muckraking. Nor do the facts sustain the existence of a business conspiracy that some muckraking magazines themselves asserted ruined them in the early twentieth century. More often these magazines suffered from chronic financial problems, staff disputes, and internal mismanagement.[22]

One of the most intriguing aspects of muckraking's decline was its concurrence with Theodore Roosevelt's 1906 speech naming the movement. Though the magazines had been filled with exposés for at least four years, no one referred to the phenomenon as muckraking until Roosevelt leveled the charge in April of that year. He first launched his attack on the investigative journalists at a March speech before the Gridiron Club, an event covered by an "off-the-record" code among politicians and reporters. President Roosevelt decided to repeat and embellish his remarks a few weeks later at a public ceremony where a cornerstone for the new House of Representatives office building was being set. Furious at muckraker David Graham Phillips's depiction of the Senate as a den of plutocrats in a series then running in *Cosmopolitan,* Roosevelt dressed the investigative reporters down for exaggerated claims, lack of goodwill, and deliberate efforts to stir up class war. In denouncing "mud slinging," Roosevelt emphasized, he did not mean to endorse "whitewashing." But Roosevelt clearly intended to upbraid the journalists harshly for what he considered literary and political excesses.[23]

Two aspects of the muckraking speech are particularly notable. The first was Roosevelt's gross misrepresentation of Bunyan's *Pilgrim's Progress.* "The Man with the Muckrake" appears very briefly in Bunyan's allegory tracing the "conversion journey" of the pilgrim through what is clearly seventeenth-century England. When the muckraker does appear, it is to demonstrate the spiritual bankruptcy of the "man of this world" who worships material things that "carry . . . hearts away from God." The Interpreter equates the "riches" of the world slavishly focused on by the muckraker with worthless "straws and sticks and dust." "The President," Ida Tarbell once acerbically noted, "would have been nearer Bunyan's meaning if he had named the rich sinners of the times who in his effort to keep his political balance he called 'malefactors of great wealth'—if he had called them 'muckrakers of great wealth' and applied the word 'malefactors' to the noisy and persistent writers who so disturbed him." In choosing a passage from *Pilgrim's Progress* Roosevelt selected a text that was widely read in the United States and would have evoked instant associations to Christianity and morality. In so doing, he took the moral high ground from the reporters with a rhetorical flourish that overnight became headline news.[24]

The second interesting dimension of Roosevelt's attack on the muckrakers was that it proved extremely effective politically. Although he later explained to Steffens, Baker, and S. S. McClure that he was thinking of Phillips and his ilk rather than the responsible writers for *McClure's*, he made no such distinction in his speech. Editorials across the nation endorsed the reasoned and balanced tone of the speech. Most important, the muckrakers themselves seemed embarrassed by the president's assault on their work. Tarbell had hoped her work on Standard Oil "might be received as a legitimate historical study, but to my chagrin I found myself included in a new school, that of the muckrakers." Roosevelt's had been "a typically violent speech," Tarbell later wrote, and "the conservative public joyfully seized the name." There is no question that Tarbell took the attack personally, and little doubt that she changed her emphasis because of its sting. "This classification of muckraker, which I did not like, helped fix my resolution to have done for good and all with the subject which had brought it on me."[25]

Ray Stannard Baker seemed equally hurt to be labeled a "muckraker." "It was difficult for me to understand this attack," he later admitted, "considering all that had recently happened, all that the President owed to investigations and reports of at least some of the magazine writers . . . the many letters of approval he had written regarding the work I had been doing." The speech left Baker "anxious and indignant," even "fearful that such an attack might greatly injure the work which we were trying to do." Baker wrote a thoughtful letter to Roosevelt emphasizing the importance of the right to freedom of the press. "The first to stop," he told the President, "will be those who have been trying honestly to tell the whole truth, good and bad, and leave the field to the outright ranters and inciters." Baker's comment proved remarkably predictive. For the three writers who brought fame to *McClure's Magazine,* muckraking began to die the day Roosevelt characterized as pedestrian, immoral, and even dangerous a movement that had become for Tarbell, Steffens, and Baker a calling, a profession, and a driving social responsibility.[26]

In another sense, of course, muckraking never died. In the early twentieth century Steffens, Tarbell, and Baker helped advance a hard-hitting, socially conscious, independent, and factual investigative journalism. Their example changed journalism, shaped public opinion, and enlivened American politics. If their fascination with individuals and their faith in the collective power of

American citizens seems sadly dated by some modern standards, we should not lose sight of the sense of "fine anticipation," in Lippmann's words, that informed their work. Richard Hofstadter once wrote: "A civilization that needs sob-sister journalism is a sad one, but the same civilization incapable of producing it would be worse."[27] In 1906 a hurt and humiliated Ray Stannard Baker seemed to find some comfort in a similarly ironic sense of history. On a lonely December day he wrote in his diary: "When there arise men who cry out ... your politics are rotten, your legislatures are corrupt, your business is immoral, you turn on them, not answering them with arguments and call them pessimists and *muckrakers*. By and by after they are dead and don't care, you may discover that some of them are prophets."[28]

NOTES

[1]Louis Filler, *The Muckrakers* (University Park, Pa.: Pennsylvania State University Press, 1976); Kathleen Brady, *Ida M. Tarbell: Portrait of a Muckraker* (New York: Sea View/Putnam, 1984); and C. C. Regier, *The Era of the Muckrakers* (Chapel Hill, University of North Carolina Press, 1932), chaps. 3–5, are examples.

[2]Robert B. Downs, Afterword, in Upton Sinclair, *The Jungle* (New York: New American Library, 1980), 349; Richard L. McCormick, "The Discovery That Business Corrupts Politics: A Reappraisal of the Origins of Progressivism," *American Historical Review* 86 (1981): 265–67; Ray Stannard Baker, *American Chronicle: The Autobiography of Ray Stannard Baker* (New York: Charles Scribner's Sons, 1945), chap. 21; Robert C. Bannister, *Ray Stannard Baker: The Mind and Thought of a Progressive* (New Haven: Yale University Press, 1966), 96–102.

[3]Brady, *Ida M. Tarbell*, 129–30; Daniel Yergin, *The Prize: The Epic Quest for Oil, Money, and Power* (New York: Simon and Schuster, 1992), chaps. 2, 4, 5; Morton Keller, *Affairs of State: Public Life in Late Nineteenth Century America* (Cambridge: Harvard University Press, 1977), 522–31; Bannister, *Ray Stannard Baker*, 96.

[4]Examples are Gabriel Kolko, *The Triumph of Conservatism* (Chicago: Quadrangle Books, 1963), 15–16, 111–12, 160–61; Samuel P. Hays, "The Politics of Municipal Reform in the Progressive Era, *Pacific Northwest Quarterly* 55, no. 4 (October 1964); John Chamberlain, *Farewell to Reform* (Chicago: Quadrangle Books, 1965).

[5]Chamberlain, *Farewell to Reform;* Kolko, *Triumph of Conservatism;* David M. Chalmers, *The Social and Political Ideas of the Muckrakers* (New York: Citadel Press, 1964), 140–41.

[6]Kolko, *Triumph of Conservatism,* 161; Frank L. Mott, *A History of American Magazines* (Cambridge: Harvard University Press, 1957), 4:208–9; Harold S. Wilson, *McClure's Magazine and the Muckrakers* (Princeton: Princeton University Press, 1970); Regier, *Era of the Muckrakers.*

[6]Kolko, *Triumph of Conservatism,* 161; Mott, *History of American Magazines,* vol. 4: 208–9; Wilson, *McClure's Magazine,* Regier, *Era of the Muckrakers.*

[7]"The Muck-Rake versus the Muck," *The Arena* 35, no. 199 (June 1906): 625.

[8]Brady, *Ida M. Tarbell,* 152.

[9]*The Nation,* 5 January 1905, 15.

[10]Yergin, *The Prize,* 105.

[11]George Alger, "The Literature of Exposure," *Atlantic Monthly,* August 1905, 210–11.

[12]"The Literature of Exposure," *The Independent,* 22 March 1906, 690–91.

[13]Mott, *History of American Magazines* 4:599; Wilson, *McClure's Magazine,* 64–65; Chalmers, *Social and Political Ideas,* 11; Thomas C. Leonard, *The Power of the Press* (New York: Oxford University Press, 1986).

[14] Ida M. Tarbell, *All in the Day's Work* (New York: Macmillan, 1939), 247–53; Brady, *Ida M. Tarbell,* 159.

[15] Baker, *American Chronicle,* 183–84, 172.

[16] Bannister, *Ray Stannard Baker,* 94–102.

[17] Stone, quoted in Justin Kaplan, *Lincoln Steffens: A Biography* (New York: Simon and Schuster, 1974), 143; see also 126, 139–43.

[18] Ernest R. May, "American Imperialism: A Reinterpretation," in *Perspectives in American History,* ed. Donald Fleming and Bernard Bailyn (Cambridge, Mass.: Charles Warren Center for Studies in American History, Harvard University, 1967), 1:135–53; McCormick, "Discovery."

[19] William Kittle, "The 'Interests' and the Magazines," *Twentieth Century* 2, no. 8 (May 1910): 124–25.

[20] Walter Lippmann, *Drift and Mastery* (New York: Mitchell Kennerly, 1914), 4, 19, 9. For a superb historical analysis that demonstrates Lippmann's view, see McCormick, "Discovery."

[21] Mott, *History of American Magazines* 4:207–9, 599–607; Tarbell, *All in the Day's Work,* 281; Bannister, *Ray Stannard Baker,* 112; Kaplan, *Lincoln Steffens,* 164.

[22] Mott, *History of American Magazines* 4:209; Chamberlain, *Farewell to Reform,* 140–41; Wilson, *McClure's Magazine;* Hofstadter, *Age of Reform* (New York: Vintage, 1955), 195–96; Michael Marcaccio, "Did a Business Conspiracy End Muckraking? A Reexamination," *The Historian* 47, no. 1 (November 1984).

[23] John E. Semonche, "Theodore Roosevelt's 'Muck-Rake Speech': A Reassessment," *Mid-America* 46, no. 2 (April 1964); Arthur and Lila Weinberg, *The Muckrakers* (New York: Simon and Schuster, 1961), 58–59.

[24] John Bunyan, *The Pilgrim's Progress* (Guildford, England: Lutterworth Press, 1974), 197–98; Tarbell, *All in the Day's Work,* 242; Anne Laurence, W. R. Owens, and Stuart Sims, eds., *John Bunyan and His England, 1628–88* (London: Hambledon Press, 1990); Christopher Hill, *A Tinker and a Poor Man: John Bunyan and His Church, 1628–1688* (New York: Knopf, 1989), chap. 18.

[25] Semonche, "Theodore Roosevelt's 'Muck-Rake Speech,'" 124–25; Tarbell, *All in the Day's Work,* 241–42.

[26] Baker, *American Chronicle,* 203.

[27] Hofstadter, *Age of Reform,* 190, n. 2.

[28] Baker quoted in Bannister, *Ray Stannard Baker,* 106.

A Brief Chronology of the Muckraking Years (1890–1912)

1890: Publication of police photographer and journalist Jacob Riis's *How the Other Half Lives,* an exposé of living and working conditions in New York City's slums.

The two major women's suffrage organizations are merged into the National American Woman's Suffrage Association as Wyoming enters the union as the first state providing full voting rights for women.

General Federation of Women's Clubs formed, creating a national network of reform-minded women who soon turn their attention to social welfare reform.

Sherman Antitrust Act passed to prevent monopolies in restraint of trade. The legislation appeared to make impossible the formation of trusts or other large business organizations that would seek to monopolize trade and commerce. However, weak enforcement and narrow judicial interpretation undermine the impact of the legislation.

Massacre of Sioux Indians by U.S. Seventh Cavalry Division takes place in Wounded Knee, South Dakota, in one of the last nineteenth-century military engagements of American Indians and white soldiers.

1892: The Populists organize a political party, the People's Party; issue a platform calling for widespread social, economic, and political reform; nominate James B. Weaver for President; and win more than a million votes.

Standard Oil of New Jersey is formed.

Violent strike at the Carnegie-owned Homestead Steel Works in Pennsylvania and in the mines of Coeur d'Alene, Idaho.

Grover Cleveland elected president.

1893: A financial panic ushers in four years of economic depression marked by widespread unemployment, plummeting agricultural prices, and thousands of business failures.

World's Columbian Exposition in Chicago celebrates the rise of modern technology, advances in literature, culture, and the arts.

McClure's Magazine begins publication.

Maggie: A Girl of the Streets, Stephen Crane's bleak novel depicting the harshness of urban life, is published.

1894:   Jacob S. Coxey organizes a march of several hundred unemployed—Coxey's Army—on Washington to demand jobs and currency inflation from the federal government.

An American Railway Union–led strike follows wage cuts at the Pullman Palace Car Company in Chicago and leads to widespread shut-downs of railroads. President Cleveland issues a federal injunction against the strike and orders in federal troops; ARU leader Eugene V. Debs is arrested and imprisoned.

National Municipal League is formed in an effort to clean up city government. The league was one of many Progressive-era voluntary organizations formed in response to late-nineteenth-century urban problems.

Lexow Commission investigates police corruption in New York City.

Henry Demarest Lloyd publishes *Wealth against Commonwealth,* a scathing attack on monopolies such as the Standard Oil Company.

1895:   The Supreme Court rules in *U.S. v. E. C. Knight* that the Sherman Act does not apply to American Sugar Refining Company, a corporation widely known as the "sugar trust" that monopolized sugar refining.

In *Pollack v. Farmers' Land and Trust Co.,* the Supreme Court rules the income tax is unconstitutional.

A price war among the popular magazines leads to ten-cent periodicals.

Tarbell's "Early Life of Lincoln" appears in *McClure's Magazine.*

1896:   *Plessy v. Ferguson* results in the infamous "separate but equal" Supreme Court decision upholding the constitutionality of racial segregation.

After a tumultuous campaign, Republican William McKinley defeats the Democratic and Populist candidate William Jennings Bryan and is elected president.

1898:   Battleship *Maine* is sunk in Havana harbor, Cuba; Hearst newspapers whip up war sentiment.

Spanish-American War.

Theodore Roosevelt leads his Rough Riders up San Juan Hill with accompanying ballyhoo in the press.

United States acquires Puerto Rico, Guam, and the Philippines and annexes Hawaii as Congress engages in fierce debate over imperialism.

Ray Stannard Baker begins working at *McClure's Magazine.*

1899:   National Consumers' League formed to press for better working conditions.

Thorstein Veblen publishes *The Theory of the Leisure Class,* analyzing the social and cultural irrationality of American capitalism.

1900: International Ladies' Garment Workers Union founded.

Robert M. La Follette elected governor of Wisconsin, ushering in an administration marked by broad legislative reform in the state.

Lincoln Steffens joins *McClure's Magazine* as managing editor.

William McKinley reelected to the presidency.

Sister Carrie, Theodore Dreiser's tale of a country girl adrift in a brutal and exploitative city, is published.

1901: U.S. Steel, first billion-dollar corporation, formed.

Socialist Party of America organized.

Theodore Roosevelt becomes the youngest president in U.S. history after William McKinley is assassinated by an anarchist.

Frank Norris's brutal fictional account of the railroads' oppression of wheat growers, *The Octopus,* is published.

1902: Anthracite coal strike in the mining regions of Pennsylvania.

Roosevelt initiates antitrust action against the Northern Securities Company.

Newlands Act earmarks funds from public land sales for irrigation and development projects in the West.

1903: *McClure's Magazine* publishes famous January issue with a selection of Steffens's *The Shame of the Cities,* Tarbell's *History of the Standard Oil Company,* and an essay by Ray Stannard Baker, "The Right to Work."

Women's Trade Union League founded to encourage cross-class alliances among working-class women and middle-class reformers, to advance the organization of women workers into unions, and to lobby for improved working conditions.

Bureau of Corporations formed within the Department of Commerce and Labor to monitor and investigate corporation conduct in interstate commerce.

W. E. B. Du Bois publishes *The Souls of Black Folk,* a meditation on race in post-Reconstruction America.

1904: Lincoln Steffens publishes *The Shame of the Cities.*

Ida M. Tarbell's *History of the Standard Oil Company* appears in book form.

In *Northern Securities Company v. United States,* the government wins its antitrust suit against a railroad holding company under the provisions of the Sherman Antitrust Act.

Theodore Roosevelt elected president.

1905: Under the leadership of W. E. B. Du Bois, the Niagara Movement is launched in an effort to end racial discrimination and segregation and advance the civil rights and economic equality of African Americans.

In *Lochner v. New York,* the Supreme Court strikes down a New York State law setting maximum hours for bakers.

Industrial Workers of the World (IWW) formed with the radical promise of mass mobilization of industrial workers into one big union.

1906: Ida Tarbell, Lincoln Steffens, Ray Stannard Baker, and John Phillips leave *McClure's* to join the *American Magazine.*

Upton Sinclair's brutal exposé of the meat packing industry, *The Jungle,* is published.

Roosevelt criticizes the muckrakers in a speech while laying a cornerstone for the new House of Representatives building.

Meat Inspection Act and the Pure Food and Drug Act win passage in Congress.

Also passed is the Hepburn Act, widening the government's regulatory powers over the railroads.

Roosevelt administration sues the Standard Oil Company of New Jersey, a holding company for Standard Oil's vast interests, charging that it has conspired to restrain trade in violation of the Sherman Antitrust Act.

1907: Financial panic shakes the economy as banks fail, industrial production lags, and unemployment soars.

1908: Republican William Howard Taft elected president, defeating Democratic nominee William Jennings Bryan and Socialist Eugene V. Debs.

The Supreme Court, swayed in part by the sociological jurisprudence informing a brief submitted by Louis Brandeis, upholds the constitutionality of an Oregon statute regulating the hours of labor for women workers in *Muller v. Oregon.*

In the Danbury Hatters case, the Supreme Court rules that the Hatters Union boycott in Danbury, Connecticut, constitutes a restraint of trade under the Sherman Antitrust Act.

White House holds a Conservation Conference to further explore the safeguarding of natural resources.

1909: National Association for the Advancement of Colored People (NAACP) founded.

Herbert Croly publishes *The Promise of American Life,* an influential call for national government activism and a reinvigoration of public life.

Ballinger-Pinchot Controversy over government misuse of public land sales for corporate profit erupts, pitting Secretary of the Interior Richard A. Ballinger against Gifford Pinchot, head of the U.S. Forest Service.

1910: Taft administration pursues antitrust campaign against key monopolies.

Mann-Elkins Act passes, placing telegraph and telephone companies under the jurisdiction of the Interstate Commerce Commission.

Woodrow Wilson elected governor of New Jersey.

In a speech that signals his reemergence into politics and his dissatisfaction with the Taft administration, Theodore Roosevelt puts out a call for a "New Nationalism" that will use the power of the federal government to advance and protect "the public welfare."

1911: A tragic fire at the so-called fireproof Triangle Shirtwaist Factory, which employed mostly women, takes the life of 146 factory workers. The International Ladies' Garment Workers Union redoubles its organizing efforts, and after lengthy investigative hearings, the New York State legislature eventually passes regulatory measures to improve factory conditions.

The Supreme Court upholds the antitrust action of the U.S. government against the Standard Oil Company of New Jersey in a decision that affirms a lower court decision mandating dissolution of the company.

1912: The new Progressive Party meets, writes a platform calling for women's suffrage, election reforms, corporate regulation, a minimum wage for women workers, and a variety of other social welfare measures and nominates Theodore Roosevelt for president.

Democrat Woodrow Wilson defeats Theodore Roosevelt in an election that garners Socialist nominee Eugene V. Debs nearly 900,000 votes.

Wilson's appeal for a "New Freedom" soon ushers in a period of intense legislative reform.

Suggestions for
Further Reading

BY RAY STANNARD BAKER, LINCOLN STEFFENS, AND IDA TARBELL

Ray Stannard Baker. *American Chronicle: The Autobiography of Ray Stannard Baker*. New York: Charles Scribner's Sons, 1945.

————. "The Color Line in the North." *American Magazine* 65 (February 1908).

————. "Following the Color Line." *American Magazine* 63 (April 1907); 64 (May–August 1907).

————. "The Negro's Struggle for Survival in the North." *American Magazine* 65 (March 1908).

————. "Organized Capital Challenges Organized Labor." *McClure's* 23 (July 1904).

————. "The Reign of Lawlessness." *McClure's* 23 (May 1904).

————. "What Is Lynching?" *McClure's* 24 (January–February 1905).

————. "What the United States Steel Corporation Really Is and How it Works." *McClure's* 18 (November 1901).

————. "When Capital and Labor Hunt Together." *McClure's* 21 (September 1903).

Lincoln Steffens. *The Autobiography of Lincoln Steffens*. New York: Harcourt Brace, 1931.

————. "Breaking into San Francisco." *American Magazine* 65 (December 1907).

————. "Enemies of the Republic." *McClure's* 22 (March 1904).

————. "Hearst, the Man of Mystery." *American Magazine* 63 (November 1906).

————. "It: An Exposition of the Sovereign Political Power of Organized Business." *Everybody's* 23–24 (September 1910–March 1911).

————. "Philadelphia: Corrupt and Contented." *McClure's* 21 (July 1903).

————. "Pittsburgh: A City Ashamed." *McClure's* 21 (May 1903)

————. "Rhode Island: A State for Sale." *McClure's* 24 (February 1905).

————. "Roosevelt—Taft—La Follette." *Everybody's* 18 (June 1908).

————. *The Shame of the Cities.* New York: McClure, Phillips, 1904.

Ida M. Tarbell. *All in the Day's Work.* New York: Macmillan, 1939.

————. "Commercial Machiavellianism." *McClure's* 26 (March 1906).

————. *History of the Standard Oil Company.* 2 vols. New York: Macmillan, 1904.

————. "Hunt for the Money Trust." *American Magazine* 75 (May 1913).

————. "John D. Rockefeller; a Character Sketch." *McClure's* 25 (July–August 1905).

————. *The Life of Abraham Lincoln.* 2 vols. New York: Macmillan, 1917.

————. "The Mysteries and Cruelties of the Tariff." *American Magazine* 71–72 (November 1910–October 1911).

————. "Rockefeller vs. Roosevelt." *American Magazine* 65 (December 1907–February 1908).

————. "What Kansas Did to the Standard Oil Company." *McClure's* 25 (October 1905).

————. "What the Standard Oil Company Did in Kansas." *McClure's* 25 (September 1905).

SELECTED WORKS ON THE MUCKRAKERS AND MUCKRAKING

Robert C. Bannister. *Ray Stannard Baker: The Mind and Thought of a Progressive.* New Haven: Yale University Press, 1966.

Kathleen Brady. *Ida M. Tarbell: Portrait of a Muckraker.* New York: Sea View/Putnam, 1984.

David M. Chalmers. *The Social and Political Ideas of the Muckrakers.* New York: Citadel Press, 1964.

John Chamberlain. *Farewell to Reform.* Chicago: Quadrangle Press, 1965.

Louis M. Filler. *The Muckrakers.* University Park, Pa.: Pennsylvania State University Press, 1976.

Richard Hofstadter, *The Age of Reform.* New York: Vintage, 1955.

Justin Kaplan. *Lincoln Steffens: A Biography.* New York: Simon and Schuster, 1974.

Walter Lippmann. *Drift and Mastery.* New York: Mitchell Kennerly, 1914.

Peter S. Lyon. *Success Story: The Life and Times of S. S. McClure.* New York: Charles Scribner's Sons, 1963.

Richard L. McCormick. "The Discovery That Business Corrupts Politics: A Reappraisal of the Origins of Progressivism." *American Historical Review* 86 (1981).

Michael Marcaccio. "Did a Business Conspiracy End Muckraking? A Reexamination." *The Historian* 47, no. 1 (November 1984).

Frank L. Mott. *A History of American Magazines.* 5 vols. Cambridge: Harvard University Press, 1938–1968.

C. C. Regier. *The Era of the Muckrakers.* Chapel Hill: University of North Carolina Press, 1932.

John E. Semonche. "Theodore Roosevelt's 'Muck-Rake Speech': A Reassessment." *Mid-America* 46, no. 2 (April 1964).

Upton Sinclair. *The Brass Check.* Pasadena: Privately printed, 1919.

Arthur and Lila Weinberg. *The Muckrakers.* New York: Simon and Schuster, 1961.

Harold S. Wilson. *McClure's Magazine and the Muckrakers.* Princeton: Princeton University Press, 1970.

SELECTED WORKS ON THE HISTORICAL CONTEXT

Martin K. Bulmer, Kevin Bales, and Kathryn Kish Sklar. *The Social Survey in Historical Perspective, 1880–1940.* Cambridge: Cambridge University Press, 1991.

Alfred D. Chandler. *The Visible Hand: The Managerial Revolution in American Business.* Cambridge: Harvard University Press, 1977.

Melvyn Dubofsky. *Industrialism and the American Worker, 1865–1920.* Arlington Heights, Ill.: AHM Publishing Corp., 1975.

Herbert G. Gutman. *Work, Culture, and Society in Industrializing America.* New York: Vintage, 1977.

Samuel P. Hays. *The Response to Industrialism, 1885–1914.* Chicago: University of Chicago Press, 1957.

Morton Keller. *Affairs of State: Public Life in Late Nineteenth Century America.* Cambridge: Harvard University Press, 1977.

Alexander Keyssar. *Out of Work: The First Century of Unemployment in Massachusetts.* Cambridge: Cambridge University Press, 1986.

Gabriel Kolko. *The Triumph of Conservatism.* Chicago: Quadrangle Books, 1963.

Michael E. McGerr. *The Decline of Popular Politics.* New York: Oxford University Press, 1986.

David Montgomery. *The Fall of the House of Labor: The Workplace, the State, and American Labor Activism, 1865–1925.* Cambridge: Cambridge University Press, 1987.

Nell Irvin Painter. *Standing at Armageddon: The United States, 1877–1919.* New York: Norton, 1987.

Theda Skocpol. *Protecting Soldiers and Mothers: The Political Origins of Social Policy in the United States.* Cambridge: Harvard University Press, 1992.

Stephen Skowronek. *Building the American State: The Expansion of National Administrative Capacities, 1877–1920.* Cambridge, Eng.: Cambridge University Press, 1982.

Jon C. Teaford. *The Unheralded Triumph: City Government in America, 1870–1900.* Baltimore: John Hopkins University Press, 1984.

Robert H. Wiebe. *The Search for Order, 1877–1920.* New York: Hill and Wang, 1967.

Index